Which of the following companies offer health-care benefits for domestic partners of the same sex?

a) Apple Computer Inc.

b) Ben & Jerry's Homemade Inc.

c) MCA, Inc.

d) Federal National Mortgage Association

Which of the following companies have a policy that forbids discrimination based on sexual orientation?

a) American Telephone & Telegraph Co. (AT&T)

b) Colgate Palmolive Co.

c) Harley Davidson Inc.

d) Bank of America

Which of the following companies include awareness of gay and lesbian issues in their training programs?

a) U.S. West

b) Digital Equipment Corp.

c) International Business Machines Corp. (IBM)

d) Arizona Public Service

Answers: All of the above. For more information, see the listings inside.

THE
100
BEST COMPANIES
FOR
GAY MEN
AND
LESBIANS

ED MICKENS

EDITOR AND PUBLISHER,
Working It Out

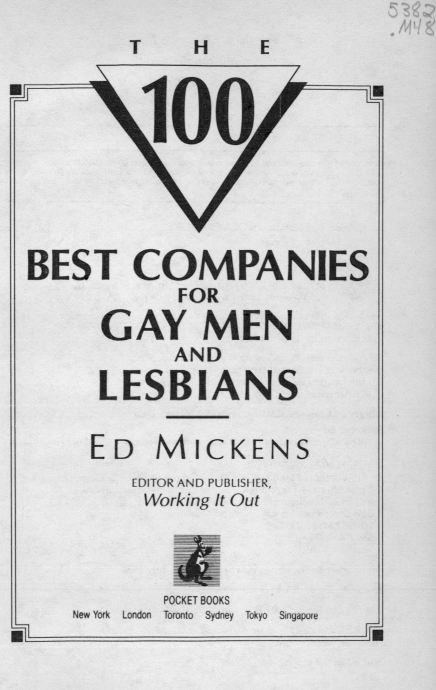

POCKET BOOKS

New York   London   Toronto   Sydney   Tokyo   Singapore

For those who have learned
(and taught me)
not to be afraid
to ask

An *Original* Publication of POCKET BOOKS

POCKET BOOKS, a division of Simon & Schuster Inc.
1230 Avenue of the Americas, New York, NY 10020

Copyright © 1994 by Ed Mickens
Cover design by Todd Radom

Library of Congress Cataloging-in-Publication Data

Mickens, Ed.
    The 100 best companies for gay men and lesbians / Ed Mickens.
      p.   cm.
    ISBN 0-671-87479-9
    1. Vocational guidance for gays—United States. 2. Corporations—United States—Directories. 3. Job hunting—United States.
4. Gays—Employment—United States. I. Title. II. Title: 100 best companies for gay men and lesbians.
HF5382.M48   1994
338.7'4'02573—dc20   94-6133
                                       CIP

First Pocket Books trade paperback printing July 1994

10 9 8 7 6 5 4 3 2 1

Design: Stanley S. Drate/Folio Graphics Co. Inc.

POCKET and colophon are registered trademarks of Simon & Schuster Inc.

Printed in the U.S.A.

CONTENTS

II

COMPANIES

CONTENTS

III

TALENT

ACKNOWLEDGMENTS

There are literally hundreds of people who have made this book possible. Forgive me if I can't name you all. I include here all the subscribers, friends, supporters, and correspondents of *Working It Out: The Newsletter for Gay and Lesbian Employment Issues*, and the other courageous people, gay and not, whom I have met while trying to make change in the workplace *and* keep track of it. Thanks.

For specific help in creating this book, I need to thank Dana Isaacson, my editor, and Bill Grose at Pocket Books; Barbara Lowenstein, my agent; Michael Fernandez, for his research assistance; Kathy Hinckley for her technical wizardry; and Joan Weingarten, for being the Christmas angel.

For their inspiration, insights, and information, I am indebted to Jerri Allyn, Simon Billenness, Steve Caramia, Alan Dee, Paula Ettelbrick, Ann Evans, Bobbie Friedman, Marguerite Heilman, Eric Hyde, Mark Kaplan, Per Larson, Jay Lucas, Grant Lukenbill, Joe McCormack, Brian McNaught, Chip Tharsing, Angela Van Patten, and Linda Workman.

In that most special category of appreciation, for those who not only assisted in many of the above-mentioned ways but also have so generously given their unquestioning moral (and often material) support: Linda Konstan (certainly the fairy godmother of this book, if she'll forgive me the term) and Rob Brading; Mary Rivera and Fred Velez; Peg Streep (goddess of practicality) and Peter and Alexandra Israel; Steve Goldstein and Jim Saslow; Mary Alice Molloy, editor extraordinaire; Stephanie Blackwood; Robert Canacari; Ed Tighe; my teacher Ellen Solart; Frank Boros and the rest of my teammates, Susan Baum, Susan Berton, Jacques Germans, Mary Kuechler, and Jan McLean. Thanks for teaching me what family is all about.

Finally, I'd like to thank my friend Alan Ross, radio host and master of the art of encouragement. His unexpected death in a fire in December 1992, while the idea for this book was being formulated, was a reminder— even for those of us who have lived through more than a decade in a senseless war zone of illness and untimely death—that the time to do it is now.

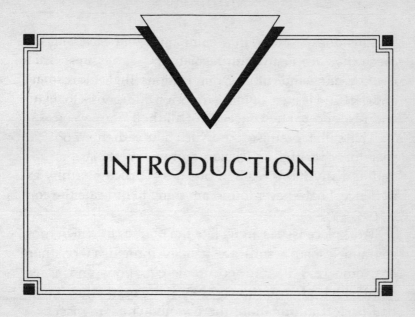

INTRODUCTION

Employers who do well addressing gay and lesbian issues are the organizations that will excel in the years to come.

Maybe I ought to repeat that.

Employers who do well addressing gay and lesbian issues are the organizations that will excel in the years to come. They will probably outshine their competitors. They will grow and develop profitably in their industries. They will find creative new ways to flourish in the uncertain marketplace of the 1990s and the new millennium beyond.

Why?

Talent. Plus openness and an ability to change.

This doesn't mean that companies will excel *only* because they are good with lesbian and gay issues. But it is a revealing indicator. Organizations that address gay and lesbian issues demonstrate a willingness to listen and respond to the concerns of all their employees.

That's the premise on which I based this book. In years of reporting on lesbian and gay workplace issues, and in many more years of business and community experience, I have never found anything to indicate the contrary.

Workplace issues aren't like the politics in which most gay and lesbian issues are usually framed. Here, there are some very definite economic equations and agreements: I'll trade you this for that. If the marketplace truly had perfect information, there wouldn't be any issues.

But we don't live in a world of perfect information. Not yet, at least. There is a great deal of fear and misunderstanding, and, apparently, there are people who would like to see these maintained.

That situation was extensively illustrated in the national media in 1993 as the U.S. military desperately contended, despite the overwhelming proof to the contrary, that lesbians and gay men did not make suitable employees. They won their battle, at least temporarily, through politics and gross manipulation of fear and ignorance.

Far less publicized was a Pentagon report, toward the end of that same year, that showed, by its own figures, that the overall quality of military recruits during 1993 declined by four percent, particularly their level of education.

Is there a connection? I'm sure they'd deny it. But few other employers today can afford the luxury of self-delusion. Anti-gay policies repel not only lesbians and gay men, but also non-gay people of talent who can hear what that says about the organization, its overall beliefs, and where it's *not* going.

Discrimination against lesbians and gay men is rampant in the American workplace today. That may come as a surprise to many managers who do not understand that silence can be the most damaging of all anti-gay policies. Silence becomes tacit permission for discrimination, and that approach is no longer acceptable. Communication is the only tool we have for correcting misinformation and misconceptions.

Those mistakes are rampant, too. It isn't the purpose of this book to correct the most basic misunderstandings about gay and lesbian lives. Ample literature is available to those who accept simplistic ideas such as that homosexuality is a deliberate choice, or that there is such a thing as a "gay lifestyle," or that any of a wide range of stereotypes is true. Consult that literature if you need it. This book requires an open mind and an ability to listen.

In October 1993, after the first Midwestern Conference on Gay and Lesbian Workplace Issues, the business section of the *Chicago Sun-Times* ran a report under the headline "Gay Employees Give Up Privacy for Work Rights."

I was startled, especially to see my own picture beneath the headline. Nothing of the sort was ever said at the conference I had spoken at. We had come together to discuss discrimination and how to eliminate it. Anything about "keeping [our] sex lives private" was assumed: we expect the same privacy as anyone else. But the reporter made her assumption, and wrote her story on that bias.

In the first part of this book, I've tried to define what lesbian and gay issues companies are facing today, what effects they have, and what solutions are available. In the second part, I identify, as a resource, the "role model" employers at different steps in the process of change. Finally, in the third part, I speak directly to my fellow gay men and lesbians—the talent—about our options and opportunities. Non-gay readers might also find this discussion useful as well—if for nothing else, as a picture of what might be coming.

Sometimes, while talking with companies and businesspeople about gay and lesbian issues, I remember that this book could not have been written before the 1990s. And I wonder if it would be similar to have been writing during the 1960s about race in the workplace. Or in the 1970s about women in the workplace. Or in the 1980s about disability in the workplace. In each case, would there have been a similar uneasiness about such a hot topic? Would there have been the same, frequent, uncertain embarrassment about not having done enough of what should be done? Would there have been the same (if only occasional) strident defensiveness—when there wasn't even any criticism?

I can't know that. But I do suspect that I would never have assembled a cast of companies and characters that I could be as proud of as the ones I celebrate here.

A NOTE ON TERMINOLOGY

Throughout this book I have used the phrase "lesbians and gay men" to denote people of same-sex orientation. I randomly reverse it so that neither gender feels slighted. "Gay and lesbian" is not meant to exclude people who identify themselves as bisexual, whose issues in the workplace overlap with ours at least half the time. The same goes for people who are transgendered, and so on. Anyone who wants to be a member of this group is certainly welcome. I sometimes use the term "gay" as a form of shorthand, as in "gay-friendly." Everyone understands what I mean, I hope.

My personal preference is, whenever possible, for the term "queer." Not on issues of feeling "empowered" by snatching back a term so frequently used against us, but because I like the traditional definition of "different." It's also gender-free, inclusive of the above groups, and more easily understood than the "Uranian" of Oscar Wilde's day. However, I have given in to the objections of (queer) friends and colleagues who still find the term offensive.

I find the term "homosexual" archaic and, well, a bit clinical, so I avoid it whenever possible. It also reinforces the idea of a strict dichotomy in human sexuality, which Kinsey (and our bisexual friends) shows to be more of a continuous spectrum. Likewise, I try to avoid the term "heterosexual." But I loathe the term "straight" with its opposite implication of "bent." Thus, I prefer using "non-gay." You know who you are.

Finally, as you've already noticed, dear reader-who-can-identify-yourself-any-way-you-like, I enjoy using the term "we" for the gay and lesbian community. Please do not misinterpret this as an "us" and "them" scenario. As a gay man, and longtime outsider, I find much power in a term that unites me with a remarkable (and feisty) group of people.

This book is intended to be safe for people of all sexual orientations.

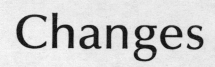

Changes

Just what makes a gay-friendly company?
How does it get that way?
Why is that important?

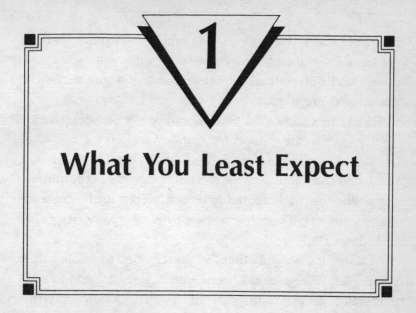

1

What You Least Expect

NEW YORK/DETROIT
SUMMER 1993

When your primary focus is on finding companies with gay-friendly policies, there's a great temptation to stereotype. I admit it: I was doing it too. I mean, some employers just seemed so *unlikely*. Especially those that came from industries completely imprisoned by their own rigid (and unfriendly) self-images, or organizations loaded with almost legendary horror stories from gay and lesbian employees, or companies that had done something so incredibly (and stupidly) *bad*.

It was a mistake to think like this, partly because it ignores the very forces of change that I find myself researching and writing about. (Dummy! Give up the old pro-gramming!) But mostly, because it underestimates the power and determination that lesbians and gay men will put toward progress.

A phone call helped pull me out of my self-delusions.

I pick up the phone. A man's voice greets me cau-tiously—it's a management-type voice. He gives me his name and the name of who referred him to me (a prominent gay politico—I'm delighted to be considered useful by such exalted circles). Then the name of his company; it's Gen-eral Motors.

Oh, no! It's not only that I've gotten used to finding that companies whose names begin with "General" tend to take it literally, keeping anti-gay policies in lockstep with the Pentagon. It's the instant image I get of GM: an infamous promotional video they produced in 1991. In it, they com-pared their pickup with a competitor's (which, perhaps not coincidentally, was Japanese). The competitor's was referred to as that "little faggot truck." When the promo was shown at a press conference, it caused a minor scandal in the indus-try media, which briefly spilled over into the gay/lesbian press, and then the general news. The company got tens of thousands of letters in protest (including at least one, from a gay colleague of mine, threatening to return his own newly bought GM pickup). The uproar eventually died down. But the impression left was that GM didn't have a clue that it had given offense.

If my caller senses my hesitation, he says nothing. He tells me what he does at GM. He is a highly placed execu-tive, in the top few percent of management within a pyramid hierarchy where hierarchy means a lot. And then he tells me that, just a few weeks ago, he chose to come out.

Wow, I think. *This guy has balls.* Then it quickly occurs to me how vulnerable he must be feeling. I don't bring up the infamous "little faggot truck." He does.

"I signed off on it," says my caller, of the video. That is, he approved it. *Ouch.* Yet I'm not surprised. The closet causes us to do all kinds of things destructive to ourselves and the people we love. He did what he had to do. But now he's ashamed, and, in a sense, he's looking to make amends.

The incident that caused his own change was a minor one. He was in a meeting with a human resources manager. She made a blatantly homophobic comment. Typically, as our closets program us, he swallowed the remark. After the meeting, however, back in his own office, the many years he had evaded dealing with these situations finally clashed with a growing sense of self-respect. He called her boss and complained.

Within fifteen minutes, the human resources manager was in his office, apologizing profusely. One can only imagine what was going through her mind. She was only playing to the corporate culture, after all—a culture with no great track record for women, either. Was she just trying to be one of the boys? Who would have expected . . . ?

Expected what? A slight rocking of the boat? Traditionally, according to the rules of conformity practiced in most of corporate America, a complaint puts the spotlight on the complainer, rather than the problem. This is especially so with lesbian and gay issues.

There are good reasons for anyone to complain about a homophobic comment. It's hateful and wrong. It's uncivilized, in the sense it might be offensive to somebody (all sorts of people have gay children, you know). It's potentially illegal when it becomes a pattern. This was certainly true at GM, since Detroit, like most big cities, has a law that forbids discrimination on the basis of sexual orientation. In fact, GM's own policy says the same.

Good reasons for any non-gay person to make a complaint, the way a man might stand up for an offended woman, or a white for a black. Except that rarely happens. We have colorful names for men who stand up for women, or whites for blacks, and so on. But when it comes to taking a stand against homophobia, only the exceptional non-gay person will have the courage. Why? Because they immediately attract suspicion that *they might be queer themselves*. And they don't appreciate the honor.

For a gay person in this position, there's an even more compelling reason: one's own dignity. It's a much sharper (and often painful) choice, whether to stay quiet and take the abuse or speak up in your own defense.

My caller had stayed quiet many times. He worked diligently in an environment where a common epithet, playing to stereotype, is "the clay-chipping fairies in the design department." (Which goes a long way toward explaining the "little faggot truck.") He never corrected the inaccuracy, never reacted to the slap in the face. This time he spoke up. And he told them why.

Coming out is a powerful moment of glory, as anyone who has been through the experience knows. A shift occurs. Being gay is no longer your problem. It's everybody else's.

The gay executive told not only the human resources manager, but also her boss. Using his privileged access, he personally told his peers and superiors in the rest of the corporate apex. They were surprised. Wasn't he one of them? Wasn't he being groomed for even higher position? Didn't he defy just about every stereotype they'd ever had? He tells them stories about himself, like the one about the years he wore a wedding ring, just like his partner, but slipped it off his finger when he came to work. One by one, they offer respect, if not outright support. They know this man. He isn't just a political abstraction.

On the phone, now, he tells me how the human resources manager has become a champion for diversity, inclusive of sexual orientation issues. (I hold my ever-skeptical tongue.) But he expresses concern about the full implications of what he's done. Is this the end of his hard-won career? Will he never get another promotion? Will he be out of a job? Should he think about moving on while he has the choice?

I congratulate him for what he's done. I tell him about the (admittedly fragile) network available to support him. I tell him about similar stories I've heard and that sometimes things turn out just fine. Most of all, I try to convey my admiration for his courage. I think he's glad to hear that. He takes on a tone of increasing confidence.

"I've been feeling like I have about two thousand volts of power rushing through me," he says. "It's great." And he quickly focuses on just why he'd called in the first place. "How do we start changing this corporation?"

He's serious. And he's completely prepared to do it.

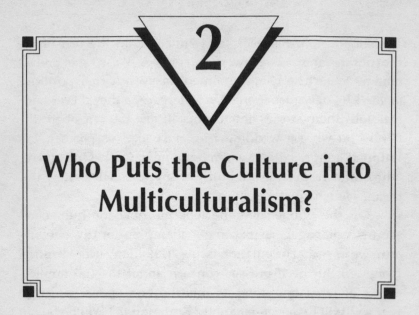

Who Puts the Culture into Multiculturalism?

Diversity has in recent years become the hot and trendy topic to talk about in business. The chief motivator is a sudden recognition of the fact that heterosexual white men are a rapidly diminishing minority within the American workforce. The less-talked-about fact that accompanies it is that most American workplaces are designed by and for white males (heterosexual, though few point it out) with little consideration for those different from that norm.

How can an organization deal with this gap? How can it make the workplace "friendlier" to the "different"—and thus make them feel more part of "the team," more productive, more trusting, more loyal, more attuned to changing markets, more . . . well, you get the idea.

The answer was "managing and valuing diversity."

Training programs that sprang up in response addressed the crucial, if obvious, point: If you're going to value and manage differences within your workforce, you need to *understand* what they are. And somewhere within the organization, there is supposed to be the assumption that this is good for the company—that it affects the bottom line— but unless top management really believes it is, this is rarely addressed. At least, tackling the first point—understanding—is progress.

Women's issues fit neatly here. Women in the workplace are subject not only to overt sexism that thwarts promotions and keeps wages below par, but also to more subtle sexism that applies a double standard toward behavior, attitude, even dress. Add to these the other stresses that working women face—most notably that they are still held primarily responsible for child care—and the situation of women in the workplace can seem to be, from a man's perspective, an entirely different "culture." Could men learn how to understand, accommodate, or even value this difference from their own reality?

"Multiculturalism" is, in fact, a term used almost interchangeably with "diversity" in many organizations. While in some companies "multiculturalism" is code for still-unresolved tensions and prejudices between blacks and whites, at least it recognizes (and openly discusses) that there is a cultural programming within each of us that informs our attitudes, expectations, and behaviors. (One of the finest diversity programs ever developed, at Digital Equipment Corporation, evolved from efforts in the 1970s to improve race relations in DEC's factories.)

The "multi" in multiculturalism shows that racial issues

in the American workplace are no longer simply black-and-white, but a complex mosaic that also includes Hispanics, Asians, Native Americans, and all sorts of other cultures and races. Indeed, the complexities within each of these groups ("Hispanic" alone varies widely; ask anyone of Puerto Rican, Mexican, Cuban, Dominican, or Spanish background) only serves to accentuate the differences within the groups we used to see monolithically as "black" and "white." African-Americans may be urban or rural in background, northern or southern or Caribbean. Whites encompass not only a multitude of ethnicities, but also religious differences, such as Jewish, Catholic, or Protestant, and so on. All affect attitudes and behaviors. So do education, political persuasion, and (the great American taboo) class.

In theory, at least, the diversity process is supposed to help us understand, respect, and appreciate one another's differences—not in the sense of some anthropological adventure (although that is sometimes involved), but to find out what makes each of us tick and how that affects our workplace behavior. For example, how traditional Asian respect for authority restrains "assertiveness." Or how "innocent" remarks can become sexual harassment. The premise is that we all need to work together, that we need to find a sense of shared purpose in a nonprejudicial environment, so that each of us may excel and the company can grow and flourish.

In the context of prevailing corporate cultures, this is a pretty revolutionary concept. But the theory is a good one and seems to work, once tolerance becomes a genuine value within the organization.

Unfortunately, even though an increasing number of companies are embracing the worthwhile idea of diversity, many are pursuing it as if it were a graduate course in affirmative action. That is, they approach it as a way of "dealing" with groups (women and racial minorities) protected under federal affirmative action laws. Revealingly, many companies stuffed a "disability" component into their diversity programs after passage of the Americans with Disabilities Act by Congress in 1991. They had to do something. Under this same way of thinking, gay and lesbian issues—since they have not yet been addressed by federal law—are left out completely.

Finding new, creative ways of addressing the problems of discrimination faced by women, racial minorities, and the disabled is commendable. But it's not diversity. There are two inherent problems. The first is that it continues to look at workers as groups, not as individuals. There's a great danger of thinking in terms of stereotypes when you take a group approach. It not only slights the differences (sometimes important) that need to be addressed within a group, but also forgets that each individual is a composite of many influences (gender, race, religion, education, age, experience, and so on). If you're practicing diversity in order to maximize each employee's productivity, cooperation, and loyalty, you have to be open and flexible enough to recognize the uniqueness of each individual and the potential that offers the workplace. (The most advanced, and successful, corporate diversity programs have learned to include issues such as "workstyle," job function—engineers are often different from salespeople—and family responsibilities.)

The second problem in confusing diversity and affirmative action is that it automatically knocks out anybody not in a preselected group, such as immigrants from countries nobody has ever heard of. Such as people with illnesses or disabilities not defined in the ADA. Such as heterosexual white men, whose anxieties about change tend to be ignored or written off as backlash. Such as gay men and lesbians, who nobody wants to talk about, or with.

If you're trying to implement a program of diversity in your organization and you're willing to acknowledge the differences of groups A, B, and C but not those of groups Q, R, and S, you're not valuing diversity. And even members of groups A, B, and C will eventually see that you're perpetrating a hoax.

Don't Ask, Don't Tell

The status of lesbians and gay men in the American workplace is the litmus test for real change in American business. Will companies recognize the essential partnership of all the people who work within them and value each for their skills, creativity, and hard work? Or will they remain loaded down with a lot of old, unproductive baggage based in prejudice, paternalism, and a sense of moral superiority? Can American business, while asking more and more from its workers in order to compete globally, acknowledge and accommodate the realities of their full lives?

We all know it has to. But control freaks will still fret about where to "draw the line." What that betrays, of course, is that there is little trust in employees, and no real tolerance.

The core problem lesbians and gay men face, especially in the workplace, is prejudice based on some uninformed belief that there is something "wrong" with us. Despite the findings of psychiatrists, psychologists, and other experts—including those of us who should know, from the empirical evidence of our own lives—there remains a persistent myth that we are somehow "morally deficient."

This idea gets frequent reinforcement from the anti-gay ranting of some religious leaders (though far from all), from the canard about being "security risks" (though even the Pentagon admits it's ridiculous), and from political types who like to brand us "anti-family" (never considering how sharply appreciative we just might be of families, since we have to work doubly hard to build and protect our own).

In the workplace, this translates into the assumption that we don't know how to behave. You saw this played out in the controversy over lesbians and gay men in the military. Politicians and military personnel who opposed the idea, perhaps feeling vulnerable about never answering why gay people are "incompatible with military service," instead treated the media to a trip to the sleeping quarters of a submarine, where bunks are "as little as two feet apart." The implication? (Nudge, nudge) Well, you know.

This may seem like an extreme example, but it occurs in other industries as well. Take advertising, for example. There seems to be an attitude that it's "okay to be gay" on the "creative" side of the business (where being gay might fall under the general stereotype of creatives being "flaky"). However, on the account-management side, the opposite is true. ("What would the clients think?") One supposes the fear is that a gay man might decide one day to walk into a client meeting dressed as Carmen Miranda.

Of course, there are many lesbian and gay sailors and advertising account managers who every day do their jobs effectively, credibly, and honorably. But policy forces them to stay in the closet, where they can eat themselves alive from shame. Where they can believe there really is something deficient about themselves.

The pervasive idea that there is something morally or behaviorally deficient in every lesbian and gay man is a lie. We've seen similar lies. It wasn't so long ago that a woman could be denied a job based on some mush about women being "not emotionally stable enough to handle it." That was a lie; now, most people see it. Similarly, racist excuses were made about African-Americans, the most euphemistic probably being "not sufficiently motivated." That was a lie; now, most people see it.

Oddly, there are plenty of supervisors who realize their employees are gay, or might be, and do a great job. But rather than face up to their own fears, they adopt an attitude—and sometimes a policy—of "Don't ask. Don't tell."

But we have to tell.

Mostly, because it's the only antidote we have for the stream of poisonous propaganda that tells us we are inferior humans. It's our chief defense, as we try to live honest, loving, productive lives, against self-loathing and self-destruction.

Yet there's another reason. The illustration was found in another one of those endless polls of "how Americans feel about gay issues." The results were mostly favorable, but that's not the point here. This poll (CBS/New York Times, 1993) subdivided respondents into two groups: those who knew a gay person, and those who did not. The pros and cons on most issues fell neatly between those two groups.

If we gay men and lesbians are to stop the evil cycle that teaches us to hate ourselves, as well as stop the encroachment on our most basic human rights, we have to educate everyone we come into contact with. We do our best education one-to-one.

So we tell.

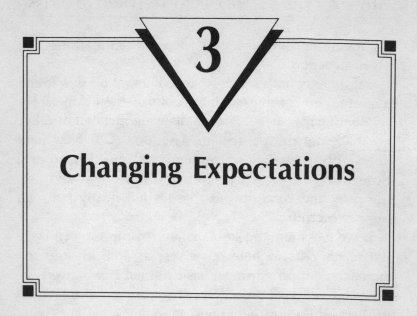

Changing Expectations

Five years ago, when I first started researching and writing about gay and lesbian business issues, it would have been impossible to write this book. Not that there weren't "gay-friendly" companies; some have good records and reputations that go back to the mid-1970s or earlier. However, few were willing to talk about it—some still won't. More significantly, few gay and lesbian employees would talk, either.

Ten years ago, the vast majority of working lesbians and gay men were grateful to have an employer who, they felt, wouldn't fire them if they were somehow, inadvertently, "found out"—seen in news coverage of a gay-rights event, entrapped by gay-hunting cops, or just becoming the subject of workplace gossip. Being "out" on the job generally meant: A) you were self-employed, B) you worked for a gay-owned business, or C) you were crazy.

We usually date the 1969 Stonewall Rebellion as the beginning of the movement for gay self-respect and social justice. Historians have traced developments back fifty years to World War II, or even a century to include Gertrude Stein, Oscar Wilde, and Walt Whitman. In all that time we learned the importance of coming out to ourselves, coming out to one another, coming out to our families, friends, neighbors, governments, churches, greengrocers, and dry cleaners. Yet . . .

It's remarkable how long we avoided coming out in the workplace, even those of us who had done all the above. In a free, capitalist system, we devalued ourselves. In a society where work is where we spend one-third to one-half our lives, we hid. In a world where one's job is a primary source of one's identity and self-worth, we lied. Work is the last big frontier. The old arguments are still common: I need this job. How else can I pay the bills? Where else could I get a job if I'm found out? For the more high-minded: I have to keep my personal life separate from my professional life.

Ah, but how long can you keep your personal life separated from your professional life when you have to put up with insulting jokes from your coworkers? When all the political talk is about ugly lies against you? When you're hiding cuts and bruises (or worse) from a gay-bashing the night before? When you're nursing a beloved whom no one knows? From a disease they say you deserve? And when the beloved dies?

You can take only so much. You can blame yourself for only so long. You can play victim only up to a point. And then you begin to feel the power you have to make change.

In the July/August 1990 issue of *Business Ethics*, a small but excellent "magazine of socially responsible business" based in Minnesota, I published an article simply entitled "The Invisible Minority: Gays and Lesbians in the Workplace." What I was trying to do was define a new sensibility I was beginning to detect in the community. I wrote:

> Gays and lesbians know a lot about silence: It is the primary, time-honored form of self-protection. The personal cost is the creation of a double life, and an often stressful juggling act to make sure the two lives don't meet. It is ironic how stable relationships and volunteer work can, under these conditions, become liabilities.
>
> When gay people are silent in their private lives, it is usually out of fear of rejection or personal harm. Silence in the workplace is justified as separating the personal from the professional—even if everybody else is talking about what they did over the weekend.
>
> Recently there has been a growing awareness of the cost of silence—an awareness that secrecy perpetuates shame, thwarts the building of community, and feeds prejudice. Among gay men in particular—a primary group devastated by AIDS—there is an equation that has become a symbol: Silence = Death.

The article continued with brief quotes from interviews with lesbians and gay men (all from the New York or San Francisco areas) who were "out" on the job, all of whom testified that they had no regrets: there were mixed reactions at their various workplaces, but the effect on their own lives was powerfully affirming. Actually, I had interviewed many more—drawn from a quiet network of personal and professional contacts—who told me the same thing, but who didn't want to be quoted in print. Those who did allow me had already been identified in the media, usually because of community-related volunteer work. That had been the source of their (willing) "outing" in the first place.

Looking at the article now, I tend to see the piece as a bit of dusty history. Its emphasis is strongly on "safety." Yes, there is also a profile on a company taking admirable steps in gay-inclusive diversity education (U.S. West, included here), a discussion about how some socially responsible investors were beginning to take an interest in how well companies were treating their lesbian and gay employees, even a mention of the importance of domestic-partner benefits. As it appeared in its edited form, the article concludes, "As companies like U.S. West and individuals . . . are discovering, making the invisible become visible may not be so frightening after all."

I remember how nervous the publisher was about running the story and still admire her courage. Yes, she did get hate mail, but not a lot. (A year and a half later, in December 1991, *Fortune* ran its celebrated cover story "Gay in Corporate America.") This was the tenth year of unrelenting gay-bashing from conservatives in Washington and the tenth year of criminal neglect of the AIDS epidemic. No one in business, or anywhere outside the lesbian and gay community, understood the angry energy percolating up after so much pressure.

My 1990 article could boast that there were two states

(Wisconsin and Massachusetts) and "nearly fifty" localities with laws that prohibit discrimination on the basis of sexual orientation and cite a researcher who predicted that "one-fourth of the U.S. population will be covered by such laws by 1995."

By 1993, there were eight states (added were California, Connecticut, Hawaii, Minnesota, New Jersey, and Vermont) and more than 160 localities with gay-rights laws. The one-fourth figure was surpassed in half the predicted time; despite noisy backlash in Oregon, Colorado, and elsewhere, institutionalized prejudice is rapidly breaking down in the face of basic human respect. In the highest court in Hawaii, even the prohibition of same-sex marriage has come under question.

The standards have changed. Safety alone isn't enough to make a gay-friendly company. Lesbians and gay men have developed enough sense of dignity that we're not grateful just to keep our jobs when the truth about our lives becomes known. We expect to be free from harassment in the workplace and expect our employers to back us up, with policy, enforcement, and training. We expect to be judged—hired, evaluated, and promoted—by the same standards as everyone else.

Furthermore, we've come to understand that we deserve equality in compensation—that means benefits. Since employers grant privileges and payments to families, we expect the same rewards accorded to our own. In 1990, I knew of only one small employer (*The Village Voice*) that offered health benefits for domestic partners of its employees, and only a sprinkling of other companies that had the decency to offer policies such as bereavement leave for the death of a partner. Today, the adoption of such policies is no longer newsworthy. Judging from the studies and negotiations going on in so many companies at the moment, they will soon be commonplace.

Am I writing too much from a New York (or San Francisco) perspective? Not entirely. The trend I describe may be most prominent in California and the Northeast Corridor, but it's occurring nationwide. The proof is in the companies listed in this book. They have changed in response to the expressed needs of their gay and lesbian employees, and they're not just in Boston or Los Angeles, but in Minneapolis and Des Moines, Seattle and Atlanta, and far-from-big cities in Vermont and (yes) Colorado.

True, there are large parts of the Midwest and the Rockies, and most of the South, where lesbians and gay men are still forced into silence by fear of local attitudes and socially permitted violence. But when I speak with them, more and more sound like the New Yorkers and Californians I interviewed in 1990. We may all be starting from different points, moving at different paces, but the direction is the same, strong and no longer reversible.

From Many, One (Sort Of)

What's most fascinating about the lesbian and gay movement for safety, acceptance, and equality in the workplace is that it's a purely grass-roots effort. There is no central organization or individual creating strategy and issuing directives. There isn't even a recognized common agenda.

There are a handful of support services that have sprung up in the past year or two, mostly informational, such as the newsletters *Working It Out* (for managers) and the *Gay/Lesbian/Bisexual Corporate Letter* (for employees); plus a small number of fine new books. A small but courageous number of corporate diversity trainers and consultants, such as the pioneering Brian McNaught, have developed education programs to tackle homophobia and heterosexism in the workplace. Groups such as Hollywood Supports have formed to lobby specific industries. (Hollywood Supports was founded by entertainment-industry types to change homophobic attitudes traditional in film. The group also created an excellent approach and information packet for negotiating domestic-partner benefits, available free to anyone.)

There have been lesbian and gay business and professional groups in major cities for nearly twenty years, yet these remain mostly social and personal-networking organizations. Even the recently formed Workplace Project of the National Gay and Lesbian Task Force is essentially a volunteer effort—most existing gay and lesbian groups are bravely struggling, within financial and personnel limitations, to cope with the overwhelming challenges of political assaults, complex court cases, AIDS, and initiating the most elementary research into lesbian and gay issues. Meanwhile, advocates on the workplace front— specialists in training, career counseling, recruitment, benefits, law, investing, marketing, and other fields—are working double-time to stay in touch with one another, just to keep up with the startling pace of progress.

The real power in this movement comes directly from

the individual lesbians and gay men in the workplace, struggling to improve their own situations. Many, if not most, work in complete isolation, unaware of any available help. I see many cases of large companies where a single, brave queer takes a stand. Sometimes this person has influence; sometimes not. Sometimes others in the company are inspired by his or her actions, and begin to band together; sometimes not. Sometimes sympathetic, non-gay colleagues or managers will become allies; sometimes not.

But it's these admirable gay and lesbian individuals who make all the difference. They are the catalysts for change, yet their actions are deeply rooted in personal survival and a striving for personal excellence. It's gratifying to hear when companies appreciate their work, as when Bob Hill, a gay manager who has shown considerable skill as an educator, negotiator, and organizer for his lesbian and gay colleagues—and who might be disdainfully considered a rabble-rouser at less perceptive companies—was given an official award for courage by his employer, DuPont.

The somewhat free-form, individual-based nature of activity on lesbian and gay workplace issues stands in marked contrast to its frequent nemesis, the radical "Christian" right, with their vast computerized mailing lists, extensive phone trees, and self-righteous, authoritarian leaders. Certainly, they can make a lot of carefully orchestrated noise whenever they suspect gay men and lesbians are being treated fairly—enough noise to keep the public relations department in a tither. But publicists are, by nature, nervous types.

When a company recognizes the legitimacy of a gay

and lesbian employee group, it's not unusual for the hate mail and calls to start flowing in, as has happened to U.S. West, Kodak, and many others. The experience is not pleasant. Some contain biblical quotes and admonitions, but others are genuinely vile. When a group of us in New York organized "Invisible Diversity" in September 1991 as the first forum for discussing lesbian and gay concerns in the workplace, we sent handsome program invitations to human resources professionals, the CEOs of Fortune 1000 companies, and similar select lists. We received an excellent response (the conference sold out), but also the following letter on plain white paper:

> TO ALL THE FAGS, GAYS, HOMOS AND LEZZIES. DO NOT MAIL ME ANY OF YOUR FAG SHIT LEZZIE HOMO PAPER WORK TO MY BUSINESS. YOU SPREAD AIDS AND GIVE THE REST OF US NOR-MAL PEOPLE A LOT OF BULL. STAY IN THE CLOSET WHERE YOU BELONG AND KEEP THE AIDS WITHIN YOUR SELVES.
>
> A NORMAL PERSON

We reproduced it on the last page of the conference workbook, in case anyone needed an illustration of the major problems that exist.

Now, this may be just the sort of thing that scares an advertiser into withdrawing sponsorship, say, from a show such as *thirtysomething*, which once had the audacity to reveal some aspects of gay reality—specifically, that two men can lie under the sheets of the same bed and talk. But we'll get to marketing and boycott issues later. In the workplace, lesbian and gay issues are almost certain to cause controversy among employees. But in these situations, it's not possible for the company to simply withdraw.

When a company sponsors homophobia-awareness training as part of its diversity effort, it's not unusual for religious radicals to demand "equal time." Fortunately, a company such as AT&T, which faced precisely this dilemma, opted for free speech. A comparison of the two "equal" programs bears its own lesson. Homophobia-awareness programs are designed to fill the void of silence in society, its media, and its schools. They fight ignorance with facts and debunk the myths and stereotypes that cause fear. A "Christian" response comes armed with familiar tracts and a familiar, scripted harangue. (I risk being called biased, but it seems to me that they're designed to maintain ignorance and inspire fear.) What really makes a difference, however, is when a trusted colleague or coworker, a friend you thought you knew, stands up and says, "I am one of you, and I am gay. What is being said is true." And they tell their own stories about living with secrecy, about their hidden lives and families, about the insults they've endured, maybe even from you, and about their fears, and how that's going to stop from now on. There is nothing that comes close to the power of that experience.

That's what gives me heart when some friends speak dejectedly of the "cultural war," and how meagerly equipped the gay and lesbian community seems to fight it. If there must be a war (and I am loath to consider it), it's not an even match. The extremists who oppose us may have the slick organizations and the money on tap and the political clout and the cloak of tradition to protect themselves, but they are trying to enforce silence and to control what they don't understand. Sure, they can (and do) make our lives miserable. But, in the long term, we have the advantage in motivation: we're fighting for what we need to survive and eventually thrive. Employers are quickly catching on that they have an interest there too.

Pressure Points

While the movement for lesbian and gay rights in the workplace could be portrayed as young and unorganized, it would be a mistake to interpret it as weak and ineffectual as well. On the contrary, workplace efforts may turn out to be the most powerful facet of the gay-rights movement in general and one of the most successful examples in the entire struggle for civil rights and human potential in our century.

The gay-rights movement, like other civil-rights movements today, is well steeped in the politics and rhetoric of the 1960s. While I have no basic disagreement with that—especially not with the link between personal liberation and social transformation—problems arise if our mind-set is too narrow to explore additional opportunities to achieve the same goals. I remember being criticized, after giving a workshop on employment issues at a gay and lesbian political conference in Washington in early 1992, for "condoning the profit motive." Somewhat surprised, I don't recall exactly how I defended my work. But I believed then, as I do now, that as long as most of us queers have to work for a living (which we do), we may as well take the opportunity to make revolution by changing our immediate environs where we can—and simultaneously changing ourselves. Gloria Steinem is right.

Gay and lesbian workplace issues aren't about politics, Washington-style. They are about personal well-being and the health and productivity of American business. In that sense, they are more about economics. This is a new perspective, so it took gay political groups and the gay media (together, the backbone of the lesbian and gay community) a while to catch on.

Yet, individual gay men and lesbians are uniquely acculturated from childhood to working in isolation. We are trained by circumstances to doubt conventional wisdom when it denies what we know is true, so we keep probing, and inventing solutions for problems no one else seems to have had before. In the workplace, as in much of gay life, we cope as long as we can, and then we take action.

The really astonishing part, however, is that people working far apart, only gradually becoming aware of one another, began to draw upon their individual skills and experiences to develop a constellation of tactics for achieving safety, acceptance, and equality in the workplace—for themselves and others in the same predicament. It looks like a comprehensive strategy, it works like a comprehensive strategy, but no one invented it or imposed it. It evolved from what seems to be a shared consciousness—an understanding of what had to be done and what could be done.

The strategy has five interrelated aspects. Each speaks

to business at a different level. Euphemistically, they are points for discussion. Often in practice they are pressure points—as needed. The five areas are: the law, employee relations, recruitment, investor relations, and marketing.

The Law

The immediate cause of the legendary Stonewall Rebellion in 1969 was gratuitous, institutionalized harassment. The New York City Police Department, like police forces across the United States, used arcane laws as an excuse to raid bars where lesbians and gay men gathered, arresting those they could collar, terrorizing those who escaped. An arrest (and your name published in the paper) simply for being in a gay establishment usually cost you your job.

Resistance to the Stonewall raid, and the three nights of riots that followed, caused New York politicians and police to back off. More important, it caused a surge of power among gay people everywhere. While "gay liberation" took many forms (including "zapping" Dick Cavett's popular TV show), its most practical and insistent focus was on changing the laws used against us. Sodomy laws, regulating private sexual acts between consenting adults (but never enforced against heterosexuals), had to be removed. But beyond this, there had to be a way of countering the profound level of discrimination lesbians and gay men faced on an everyday basis. The model existed in the antiracist civil-rights laws that had been passed nationally only a few years before.

Gay-rights laws forbid discrimination on the basis of sexual orientation. Typically, they specify the areas of housing, employment, and public accommodation. It didn't seem like an unreasonable request—still doesn't. Adoption of such laws in various jurisdictions (chiefly big cities where the gay and lesbian population was visible and politically organized) was gradual over the next twenty years, but serious backlash began to rear its head in 1977, after Dade County (Miami), Florida, passed a gay-rights bill. Anita Bryant, onetime singer and then orange-juice-pusher, spearheaded a vicious campaign of bigotry and lies that capitalized on the general population's ignorance of just who gay people are. The Miami law was repealed.

The grappling continued through the 1980s. New York City finally passed its bill in 1985, despite the hate-filled thundering of its Catholic archbishop. Houston passed, then repealed. A federal version of the bill was introduced to Congress in 1978, and although it has accumulated more than one hundred cosponsors, it has never come to a vote. The Reagan-Bush years made gay-bashing, along with other gross indecencies, socially acceptable if not fashionable. The frightening mystery of AIDS padded arguments against legal protection—a weird stretch of logic, but one that sold well to those who would prefer it to facts. The battles became more pitched, yet the number of gay-rights laws increased. In California, the law passed, was vetoed by the governor, then passed (and was signed) in a form that only protected employment. (Public accommodation had already been established by court decision; housing remains legally fuzzy.) New Jersey, in 1992, passed its law unanimously, with little fanfare. (The respected Eagleton poll showed that eighty-seven percent of the state's voters supported the law.) By 1993, nearly all the nation's major business centers protected their lesbian and gay workers.

Throughout this period of rapid legal change, the critical question was whether or not these laws had any real teeth. Employers, naturally, turned to their attorneys for answers. What was overlooked was the fact that a great many of the law firms serving corporate clients were themselves discriminating; job applicants with résumés that showed experience with gay and lesbian (or AIDS) issues were assumed to be queer and thus not hired. Nor did this create a congenial atmosphere for closeted attorneys in the firm, who might have experience through volunteer time with Lambda Legal Defense or other nonprofit gay-rights advocate groups. Typically, these firms told clients not to be concerned about the laws. They weren't worth the cost of a compliance program.

The shock came in 1991, with a lawsuit against a division of Shell Oil in San Francisco. Jeffrey Collins, a vice president with a sterling performance rating for nineteen years, inadvertently left a safe-sex memo in a company photocopier. His secretary found it and brought it to Collins's boss. Collins suddenly found himself with a dismal performance rating and was subsequently fired—and not for personal use of the Xerox machine. He sued on the basis of San Francisco's antidiscrimination law. He not only won but was awarded damages of $5.3 million. (Shell later settled for an undisclosed amount.)

Since compliance programs might be defined variously as a change in written policy, a memo explaining such, or a segment in management training, as well as meaningful intervention by top brass, it would seem that $5.3 million could buy an awful lot of compliance programs.

The problem with non-discrimination laws, as women and other minorities have already discovered, is it's difficult to prove they have been broken, and conservative courts are making it even tougher to do so. But other approaches have been taken, especially in jurisdictions without gay-rights laws. In Florida in 1992, a deputy sheriff who was fired after his boss (the sheriff) had him tailed off-duty and discovered he was gay sued on the basis of the state's constitutional guarantee of privacy. The jury found in his favor. In Georgia in the same year, an assistant state's attorney was fired after her boss (the state attorney general) found out that she had been married to her lesbian partner by her rabbi. (The Reconstructionist form of Judaism performs same-sex marriages.) She sued on grounds of freedom of religion. (She lost; her case is now on appeal.)

The law provides only the barest minimum of protection. And the political atmosphere is more volatile than ever. Even with a presumably gay-friendly Democratic administration, a federal gay-rights law seems as distant as ever. The outrages of the debate over lesbians and gay men in the military showed that Congress is not our friend. And we have reason to suspect the Supreme Court, which in 1986 decreed, essentially, that gay people were not protected in our bedrooms. We can only imagine its views about our workplaces.

Meanwhile, the radical right wing, finding that raising money against gays is easier than raising money against reproductive rights, multilingualism, or the separation of church and state, has devised a new tactic: laws that *uphold* discrimination on the basis of sexual orientation. "Special rights" they call them—as if the right to hold a job, despite what your boss thinks about who you make a life with, is "special." They sold their argument in some small towns in Oregon, lost narrowly statewide there, but won over Colorado (although the constitutionality of that amendment is still in question). And they promise to give legal force nationwide to their message that we *deserve* discrimination.

For more than twenty years, the law has been important to us. But, obviously, the law is not enough.

Employee Relations

The necessary complement to protective laws is education to answer fears, correct misunderstandings, and foster acceptance. Each lesbian and gay man knows the importance and effectiveness of this through personal experience with the non-gay people in their lives. It all centers on the act of coming out of the closet. Suddenly, stereotypes are exploded, prejudices are called into question, and what was only theory or politics becomes very humanly real. It has a profound effect.

There are lots of ways of coming out on the job. One of the oldest, and least pleasant or productive, is being forced through circumstances. In the not-quite-over-yet old days that might have meant an arrest, but now it can just as easily mean being spotted at a gay event or place, or even something as casual as forgetting to take something out of the photocopier. Or it can mean being "figured out"—which carries menacing overtones of harassment. Like "outing" (the media-hype furor of a few years ago that came to little—we still remain remarkably protective of our own), coming out under duress is potentially quite damaging to the person not prepared to deal with the consequences. It needs to be treated like trauma.

The more common way of coming out is a gradual process. First, it's made known to a trusted colleague. If that's successful, and especially if the colleague turns out to be an ally, hints, codes, and in-jokes get more relaxed. Others catch on, maybe talk about it, maybe to say it's okay. Behaviors may change. Maybe messages get sent that say it's not okay. Soon the whole department knows. A lot depends on just how valued the lesbian or gay colleague is. The chief problem here is that the gay or lesbian colleague doesn't know who knows, and those who know aren't sure if they're supposed to know. A lot of cautious tiptoeing and discomfort may result.

Sometimes a more direct route is taken. That can occur in a moment of confrontation, such as when a homophobic remark is made that a gay worker decides not to take—and tells why. Or it can be a more calculated decision: showing up one day with a symbol, such as a pink triangle, on the lapel; or putting a picture of your partner on your desk. These are gutsy (and empowering) moments. But they still leave a situation where non-gay colleagues feel uncomfortable about how to react. This is generally because, in our society, we don't know how to talk about sexual orientation—or race or other differences, for that matter.

But with rapidly increasing numbers of gay people choosing to get over a major fear and come out at work, rumbles occur in employee relations. People who have just taken a remarkably brave step, often after a lot of internal debate and years of repression, expect some kind of response.

Companies with a good system of communications (you know I'm not talking about E-mail here) and a track record showing they value their employees and respect their concerns are usually the ones that have the easiest transition in addressing gay and lesbian issues. Companies that *think* they have those attributes but have a tough time dealing with employees who come out should quickly realize that they've been deluding themselves.

Companies that run like dysfunctional families—harshly dogmatic, rigid, condescending, not thinking of workers as humans—are the ones that tend to react the worst. The greater their arrogance, the more likely they are to face lawsuits and a lot of bad publicity.

Frequently, these are companies with troubled histories in labor relations—either fighting with or fighting off unions. Some have already been surprised to find the unions adopting the concerns of their gay and lesbian members. A more vocal, activist stance on the part of lesbian and gay union members and organizers guarantees that this pressure will continue.

Of course, gay and lesbian workplace issues require the usual degree of give-and-take. Since it's the rare company that takes the initiative, the burden of starting the process sits squarely with lesbian and gay employees. They have to stand up, speak up, articulate what they want, and be open to negotiation. Usually, they have to do an enormous amount of education as well.

But why don't all employees just speak up? More often than not, it means they can't. In that case, the company would be wise to take a hard look at just what sort of corporate culture it has. Why do gay and lesbian employees feel unsafe? Are their jobs or careers really endangered? Be realistic. Are there managers in the ranks who let their personal beliefs determine their business behavior? Even despite company policy? If they feel free to violate one policy, are they doing it with others as well? Something is wrong in the ranks.

Likewise, companies often send out mixed messages to employees. Coors Brewing, for example, tries to portray itself as a gay-friendly company, as it glibly promotes its beer to the lesbian and gay market. Yet the owners still fund a family charitable foundation noted for its gifts to conservative groups, many with blatantly anti-gay missions. What are employees supposed to think?

Local influences certainly have an effect that can't be blamed on the company. In much of the South, the Midwest, and in small towns everywhere, it can be downright dangerous for an individual to be openly gay—and what's known in the workplace gets around fast. Even one of the gay-friendliest companies, Levi Strauss, admits it never hears about lesbian and gay employees outside its home base in San Francisco; that is, in its facilities in Georgia, Texas, New Mexico, and elsewhere. The company doesn't necessarily have a responsibility to change the intolerant environment around it (or does it?). But it can't ignore the situation, either. The company still ends up paying a price.

The bottom line in employee relations is productivity. Gay men and lesbians are not much different from their non-gay colleagues in how they interact with their employers—we just have a few additional issues. If employees are allowed to be comfortable in who they are, they won't have to waste a lot of energy pretending they are someone else. If they feel valued and appreciated, they'll give back in loyalty and the extra mile. If they can trust, they'll build better and more effective teams.

This is classic diversity theory, which no one has yet been able to quantify, but which any observant manager knows empirically. In 1993, the Families and Work Institute in New York released a survey of "what workers want" from a job. At the top of the list, considered a "very important" consideration by sixty-five percent of respondents, was "open communication." Right behind it (sixty percent) was "effect on personal/family life." Salary and wages ranked thirteenth (thirty-five percent).

Reporting on the study, *New York Times* business columnist Barbara Presley Noble noted, "The startling implication, especially for employers who have been depending on a workforce made tractable by fear: Companies that fail to factor in quality-of-employee-life issues when imposing total quality management or 're-engineering' or any other of the competitiveness-enhancing, productivity-improving schemes now popular may gain little but a view of the receding backs of their best people leaving for friendlier premises."

Recruitment

A logical corollary to the employee-relations situation shows up in employee recruitment. (Believe me, as a gay man, I've had to teach myself to use that word without trepidation. "Recruitment" is the explanation by some of our most ignorant detractors of how we replenish our numbers. Of course, non-gay people do it for us.)

Quietly, over the last few years, lesbian and gay issues have been dealt with on a very rarefied level of recruitment. Highly sought-after professionals in various industries (including computers, education, law, telecommunications, and others) have put their sexual orientation up front and walked away from offers by companies who couldn't handle it. Further, when a company is able to satisfactorily answer questions about policy and organizational attitude, gay and lesbian professionals have been able to negotiate "special" perks such as paying a domestic partner's relocation expenses or financing a new home owned jointly—standard proce dures for spouses, but almost never for same-sex couples. These don't become policy, unfortunately, and the company won't admit to them, but it demonstrates the success of men and women who have learned to value the power of their own talent.

These situations are not (yet) common, but they are increasing. I base that prediction on the sheer number of phone calls I get from total strangers, many of them highly accomplished managers, who say, "I can't work in this homophobic environment anymore. [The language is often a lot stronger.] Where's a gay-friendly place to work?" The need and determination in those calls inspired this book. Similar calls inspired Joe McCormack, a highly successful executive recruiter, to set up his own nationwide firm, based in Los Angeles, which is the first to specialize in placing talented gay men and lesbians who prefer to work where they can be out.

But the most serious recruitment issues companies will have to face are not with established professionals in mid-career. They are taking shape on college campuses.

The number of calls I get from people looking for jobs is almost matched by the calls I get from college career-placement officers. The first time I was invited to give a workshop by one of their associations, in 1992, the placement officer from a prestigious eastern university explained a problem that was bothering her.

She was trying to advise a senior and to prepare a résumé. The senior was graduating at the top of her class. She was president of a major campus group. She had done extensive community volunteer work. And she insisted on including all this in her résumé. The placement officer objected.

Can you guess the problem here? Of course. The senior was president of the university's gay and lesbian student association. The volunteer work was counseling lesbian and gay youth and assisting a local AIDS-awareness group. She was an out and proud lesbian, and any company that wanted her considerable talents would have to deal with that, right from the start. The placement officer thought this would be career suicide before the career was even launched.

I could only respond: Who has the problem here? Do you advise the student to start her career with lies and a sense of shame? Do you tell her she has to work in fear? Under what other circumstances would proven intelligence, leadership, and community involvement be so quickly diminished and hidden?

Heads bobbed throughout the crowded room. Many of the other placement officers were dealing with similar questions from other students. So were the recruitment representatives from corporations.

The education and advocacy work of the past quarter-century has made it possible for more lesbians and gay men to come out at an earlier age, in college or even before. Like all of us, they must grapple with the implications of being set apart as different, come to peace with it, then attempt to shape a life as fully integrated as possible, for their own dignity and self-respect.

There has been talk on several campuses of banning corporate recruitment efforts by companies that discriminate against gays and lesbians. This may not go anywhere. As Randy Shilts pointed out, in *Conduct Unbecoming: Gay Men and Lesbians in the U.S. Military,* there have been similar attempts to ban military recruitment on campuses, because of the military's outright discrimination. These were squashed by administrators, he says, because of pressure from the cozy financial relationships between universities and the U.S. government, especially the Pentagon.

Corporations may or may not have similar influence. But they need to be aware that they are in the spotlight on lesbian and gay issues. Companies that appear unfair, noninclusive, or just indifferent alienate more than the sizable pool of gay and lesbian talent. Thanks to the broad public discussion on gay rights throughout the 1980s and 1990s, the students today who grew up amid it have a much more sophisticated take on the issues. Intelligent non-gay students can see what's unfair and out of step with reality. They can see discrimination for the crude throwback that it is. And in their own searches for the open, responsive companies where they can invest their talent and build careers, they can read the barometers.

Investors

Where the law is not sufficient and the value of talent isn't fully appreciated, money still talks. America's stockholders recognized that in the 1970s and 1980s, when they began to band together to influence corporate policy in South Africa, Northern Ireland, the environment, and other issues. As the theoretical top of the capitalist heap (as in, "What will the shareholders say?"), they could exert pressure on management in publicly held companies, generate a lot of scary publicity, and they found that could be the catalyst for progressive change.

It was inevitable that lesbian and gay issues would become part of the overall picture, not only because we have finally reached a respectable place on the social agenda, but also because some of the shareholders are gay ourselves, or are our families and friends, or public agencies committed to non-discrimination, or institutions and individuals who understood that changing business is changing society.

In early 1990 the Interfaith Center for Corporate Responsibility began a research project at the request of some of its clients. The New York–based nonprofit is an investment adviser for a coalition of three hundred religious institutions and other organizational investors with a cumulative portfolio in excess of $500 billion, and some of its mostly moderate and liberal religious members were becoming upset with the conservative-religious assault on gay men and lesbians. They looked to how their pension funds and other assets might provide a countering effect.

The research project, conducted by ICCR research associate Donn Mitchell, focused on corporate attitudes toward gay and lesbian employees. Companies held within the portfolios and in jurisdictions with gay-rights laws were surveyed to determine which abided by those laws and did so "in a meaningful way." Most companies resisted giving out any information, and the resulting sample was so small that it was of questionable usefulness. But clearly a nerve had been struck, and an interesting new direction defined.

By 1991 the Calvert Social Investment Fund had become (largely through the efforts of analyst S. E. Gallagher) the first mainstream "socially responsible" mutual fund to include a "lavender screen" that assessed investment vehicles according to how a company treated its lesbian and gay employees. They were able to collect their information, but kept it confidential. That same year a group of volunteers in New York with various connections to the financial industry banded together with the idea that information about how publicly held corporations treated their gay and lesbian employees needed to be gathered on a massive scale and widely distributed so that all investors might know. The group called itself the Wall Street Project. Almost immediately, it had a case study on its hands of what it wanted investors to do.

In the summer of 1991 Cracker Barrel Old Country Store Restaurants, a Tennessee-based roadside chain with an unwieldy name, launched what could only be described as a witch hunt: it suddenly fired eleven employees at several locations with a chilling note on their pink slips: "Employee is gay." When questioned, the company offered an explanation that being gay violated the "family" nature of the business. To paraphrase the military, they might have said that being a lesbian is "incompatible with short-order cooking." (In my one contact with Cracker Barrel as a customer, stopping to pump some gas near a southern interstate in 1990, I distinctly recall that the only other customers in the rustic barn of a restaurant or kitschy gift shop were two other gay men.)

None of the firings took place in areas with gay-rights laws, so the employees had no legal recourse. However, a barrage of critical media attention erupted nationwide. Members of ACT-UP and Queer Nation arrived in large groups at various Cracker Barrel restaurants to stage kiss-ins and other direct-action theatricals. Most significantly, the company got an angry call from the office of Elizabeth Holtzman, comptroller of the city of New York. The comptroller supervises the pension funds and other investments of the city, and in that portfolio were more than one hundred thousand shares of Cracker Barrel stock. (It should also be added that the comptroller was then running for the U.S. Senate in a state with a considerable gay voting bloc.)

The philosophy of the Wall Street Project is not that investors should sell off or even avoid shares of gay-hostile companies; rather, they should use their voting privileges as leverage. Here was about as gay-hostile a company as one could find in the 1990s. The group worked with the comptroller's office and contacted the financial officers of other governments with gay-rights laws to look for Cracker Barrel in their portfolios and perhaps join in with a proxy. The response they received was underwhelming.

There was little time to prepare for Cracker Barrel's annual meeting in September. Enterprising ACT-UP members had bought one share each as the price of admission, but the company was prepared: anyone "suspicious" was detained, searched, and shunted to an area behind a soundproof glass wall. (So, technically, they were admitted.) Even the legal representative from the New York City comptroller's office was searched and delayed from entering the meeting, although his protests saved him from the glass booth. The meeting was quickly wrapped up before any controversy could be addressed.

Looking forward to the 1992 meeting, the comptroller's office began filing papers for a shareholders' resolution that would require the company to 1) adopt a policy that prohibits discrimination on the basis of sexual orientation and 2) reinstate the eleven fired employees. After considerable legal wrangling, the Securities and Exchange Commission decided that, in this case, it was inappropriate for stockholders to interfere with day-to-day management decisions.

Then in 1993 federal judge Kimba Wood in New York

overruled the SEC. The vote was finally held in November of that year: fifteen percent voted in favor of the proposal. But that number, according to proxy experts, shouldn't be considered by electoral standards. In fact, most consider it a gay victory. Similar votes against apartheid got eleven percent. And any vote greater than ten percent automatically places it on the voting agenda for the next year's meeting. So the process continues.

But, as is usually the case with gay and lesbian issues, outrage over the whole nasty scenario began to send out deep and strong seismic waves. More and more investors began asking questions about gay and lesbian employment policies. Their financial managers and brokers began scrambling for answers that hadn't yet been assembled. Socially responsible analysts, such as those at Franklin Research and Development in Boston, began to include a "lavender screen." Enterprising brokers, such as James M. Dean at Paine Webber in Atlanta, began offering accounts that dealt only with proven gay-friendly companies that also performed well (his list is a secret, but their performance is exceptional). Wesley Hicks, an investment adviser also in Georgia, founded his *Gales Financial Report* newsletter along the same principles. Responding to their clients, brokers at major houses (none of whose own gay and lesbian employment policies, by the way, have anything to recommend them), from A. G. Edwards to Prudential Securities, have initiated their own research.

Investing in gay-friendly companies has clearly become a worthwhile business in itself, even if "converting" gay-hostile companies hasn't worked. The effect may well be the same. This is a phenomenon that has far to go before it flowers. But don't say I didn't warn you.

Marketing

The purchasing power of lesbians, gay men, and our allies, used as a method of leveraging changes in corporate policy—if not social policy—nicely rounds out the basic options for making dialogue within the capitalist system. The "gay and lesbian market" has already been widely discussed in the pages of *The Wall Street Journal*, *Advertising Age*, and similar publications. It's certain to remain a topic for discussion through the 1990s, and deserves several books of its own.

In fact, the gay and lesbian market—-and discussion of it—has been a critical element in the forging of a national gay and lesbian community out of a variety of what could be described as "regional" communities based in major cities. Yes, there have been nationwide challenges that have galvanized lesbians and gay men across America: twelve years of an openly hostile federal administration in Washington and, perhaps most of all, the vast scale of the AIDS scourge. Networking became essential—to share information, experience, contacts—not just in the traditional gay centers, but in small towns and the rural countryside. Everybody had something at stake. None of this large-scale networking would have been possible without the telephone, electronic mail, and other products of the communications revolution that affected all business—nor without national rallies, conferences, and organizations. But the key element for welding a national community was a national lesbian and gay media, since the existing national media couldn't be relied on for regular and timely information. So an explosion occurred, especially in gay and lesbian publications. And to function, that media needed a proven market.

But I'm getting ahead of myself.

There are two ways the lesbian and gay market views itself: as a carrot and as a stick. The stick is that favored tool of political activists, the boycott. In gay terms, the boycott had its most glorious moment in the late 1970s, when Anita Bryant led her belligerent (and successful) assault against the Dade County gay-rights law. Bryant's day job was acting as spokesperson for the Florida Orange Juice Commission, and the revenge of the gay and lesbian community (and our allies) was a nationwide boycott of orange juice. Drink grapefruit, pineapple, cranberry, or squeeze your own (no fruit jokes here, please), the word went out. Whether because of declining sales, the public relations mess of the controversy, or outright vandalism (yes, there are embarrassing stories about fast spikes ripping up the frozen juice displays), Bryant lost her job. A sense of triumph prevailed. (More than a decade later, frustrated by her inability to restart her old singing career, Bryant tried to tell us it was really her ex-husband's fault or some such nonsense. But Dade County has never reinstated its law.)

In 1992, however, when the voters of Colorado just barely passed a constitutional amendment prohibiting gay-rights laws (essentially legalizing discrimination), calls for a boycott were loud but confusing. How do you boycott a state? Not go there, obviously. (And the state apparently lost millions in canceled conventions; tourism losses during one of the best ski seasons in memory were not as persuasive.) But calls to boycott any business based in Colorado befuddled everyone. Companies such as U.S. West had actually worked against the amendment. Many gay men and lesbians had been boycotting Coors for years, because of its conservative political associations. Gay employees in companies based elsewhere, but with facilities in Colorado, faced uncomfortable dilemmas when asked to travel there. Individuals and restaurants stopped buying Celestial Seasonings teas, even though the company has a gay-friendly reputation. (Its president met with boycott activists in New York. Their demands, as he perceived them, caused him to call his attorney to discuss possible extortion charges.) Much of the furor over Colorado died down when the law was put on hold as unconstitutional—years of litigation probably lie ahead—but it was hardly a triumphant moment for the boycott stick. We've also found that anti-gay forces can use the same threats, although their results don't seem any more successful than ours.

Thus, the carrot approach moves to center stage. If it weren't for fear and ignorance, many more companies would have started cultivating the lesbian and gay market years before. Simple observation would have revealed households with greater disposable income—because there are far less likely to be any children. In the case of couples, we show a high incidence of classic DINKs (double income, no kids). Double income allows for not only a higher degree of recession proofing but also greater discretionary spending on items such as travel, entertainment, food, drink, clothing, automobiles, etc., etc. Add to that the traditional (though rarely acknowledged) role of gay people in society as open-minded and influential trendsetters. (Who decorates? Who designs? Who writes? Who knows the most fashionable places to go? Who has the best parties? I know—we're treading dangerous ground here.)

And then there is the issue of brand loyalty. Like other minority groups, we remember to reward our friends. (There are still black Chicagoans who will shop only at Carson Pirie Scott and never at Marshall Field because over a generation ago Carson's integrated its workforce, while Field's resisted.) Levi Strauss and AT&T *know* they have an edge with gay and lesbian consumers, because they are well-known as gay-friendly employers. Neither has ever made any special effort to market to the gay and lesbian community. But Levi's, backed up by research that shows three-fourths of gay men specify Levi's when we buy jeans, withstood criticism when it withdrew support from the Boy Scouts because of the latter's anti-gay policies. AT&T hasn't been as brave. It lost some credibility during a lawsuit against domestic-partner benefits, but what works in AT&T's favor is that its long-distance competitors have nothing to recommend them as gay-friendly companies.

Of course, other companies have won over the gay market in different ways. The best example is Absolut vodka, which has such a solid hold that even the most surprising closet cases admit they purchase only Absolut. Carillon Imports (then Absolut's American distributor) is no star on lesbian and gay employment issues, but it has shown consistent support in another important way: in the late 1970s when the only national gay and lesbian newsmagazine, the Los Angeles–based *Advocate*, was courting mainstream, national advertisers, Absolut signed on for the back cover. The significance was not lost on the community; we needed those ad dollars to keep growing one of our crucial, but few, national institutions (especially with Anita doing her thing in Miami). More important, when AIDS suddenly appeared in the 1980s, most national advertisers withdrew in panic. Absolut stayed. Of course, it's done a lot for AIDS benefits, and it's run those fabulous campaigns with all those witty (and mostly gay) designers too. (In 1993, Absolut switched distribution to Seagram's, a company with a fine gay-friendly track record.)

Yet, those opportunities for credibility are narrowing fast. Advertising alone doesn't buy loyalty anymore. Gay-affirmative (or even gay-suggestive) ads get attention: applause from the lesbian and gay audience, hate mail from those who want to keep us locked in the closet. "Investment in the community" is expected, such as corporate sponsorship or cultural events ranging from the eminently respectable Gay Games to the outrageously wonderful Wigstock festival, or other support for the vast array of educational, legal, or social-service organizations.

Products such as Naya water have been remarkably successful in this way. Still, as a product category gets more crowded, the sophisticated and ever-skeptical lesbian and gay market takes a closer and more discerning look at newcomers. Beyond the glitzy sideshow, how do you treat our sisters and brothers who work for you?

Consider a company like Hiram Walker & Sons. (Liquor companies love us; fortunately, we also have a highly developed system of twelve-step programs such as Alcoholics Anonymous.) Hiram Walker has poured thousands into a superb promotional campaign devised by an enlightened director of niche marketing and outside lesbian and gay consultants. (Including, briefly, this writer.) But there is a fatal flaw in the program: Hiram Walker is not a gay-friendly place to work. One of the top executives even privately admitted to having some gay-bashing experience in his youth. There's a continuity in attitude: no company policy or message has ever been put forward to reassure lesbian and gay employees that it's okay to be who they are.

My general rule of thumb for companies who ask how to market to lesbian and gay consumers: *Ask your gay and lesbian employees.* They know the market. They know your products. Who else is a better fit? All the consultants in the world can't match that insight. But Hiram Walker can't do that; employees are too afraid to come out. The results will show on the bottom line.

But is it worth that little bit of effort? Where's the carrot? Here's where we get to numbers and back to the business of a proven market.

For a population that has never actually been counted, there is suddenly available a wide array of descriptive numbers. Studies show our average household income in the $50–60,000 range, well above the $36,500 national average. They show a majority of us with college degrees. They show how often we go to the movies and the health club, how often we travel to Europe or use a Platinum card. They even show our favorite candy bar. (Okay, it's Snickers.) Except for the Snickers part, it's a flattering portrait of economic success. And it makes some people very nervous.

Not that the figures aren't credible—for what they are. Some come from the highly reputable Simmons Market Research Bureau, and they cover, by definition, "readers of gay publications." That's an easily identified group, reachable through subscription lists. And the numbers do prove that a highly desirable, affluent, educated market exists among the readership of gay publications. The publications need that. But is it all of us?

Overlooked Opinions, a Chicago-based market research firm, has gone a few steps further. It has taken great pains to establish a market survey group that goes beyond publication subscribers to include participants gleaned from marches and rallies, bars and community centers, and organization members—lesbians and gay men from every part of the country, in all walks of life. In other words, they've created a sample, in the tens of thousands, that's supposed to represent the gay and lesbian community as a whole. And the profile is just as flattering.

So what's the problem?

The most obvious concern is political, about how these numbers are used. Yes, they make compelling arguments for corporate support of gay publications and organizations, even for businesses to get on friendlier terms with the gay and lesbian community—consumers and employees alike. But there's a dark, and not unreasonable, worry about how these numbers can be used *against* us. One can't help but think of Jews in Germany in the 1930s being portrayed as rich, smart, influential, and maybe just a bit too powerful. Already, the market figures on gay men and lesbians have been interpreted by bigots to portray us as an already "privileged" class that doesn't need the "special rights" of basic civil-rights protection. It worked in Colorado, and much of Oregon, and is being used in political battles around the country. Just as we're beginning to win the educational challenge—teaching that we're not automatically child molesters, traitors, antifamily, or any of the other deadly stereotypes—are we setting ourselves up with an even more danger-ous image? For people who know institutionalized preju-dice firsthand, it's not paranoid to imagine that with a slight twist in the political or economic environment we could become very popular scapegoats.

But what if the research is true?

Ah, there's the other problem. As any minority knows, when you're trying to buck the traditional wis-dom of prejudice, you have to work much harder than anyone else, and adhere to a much higher standard—because that's how you're going to be judged. And so the numbers get questioned.

Scientifically, the numbers are invalid because you can't have a "self-selected" sample. But you can't have a survey of lesbians and gay men unless they say who they are. Thus, they are "self-identified," which some would claim is self-selected. Might it be more accurate to say that these numbers represent gay men and lesbians who are "out"? Sure. Hold that thought.

The other side of the criticism about the numbers

concerns representation. It's become a pretty well-established fact that, whatever causes us to be gay, we are fully distributed through all human categories: gender, race, nationality, culture, religion, and so on. Does it also mean we're born into every economic stratum? Of course. But does it mean we *stay* economically where we're born?

Is it possible that, with the natural curiosity we have from needing to find out why we're different from everyone else, we're more likely to follow through on educational opportunities? Is it possible that, not encumbered at an early age by children and families, we can secure higher degrees? Is it possible that, without dependents or role-model pressures, we can take more risks and make more long-term investments in our careers? Is it possible that, feeling vulnerable because we're different, we work harder? Is it possible that, with our different viewpoint and unusual networks, we can take a more creative and expansive outlook on our lives?

These are the types of questions that could drive the politically paranoid wild. Granted, they could all be tossed aside with a cause-and-effect answer: the numbers show that it's easier to be a self-identified homosexual when you're economically secure. But the reverse could also have some truth to it: once you have come to terms with being gay—to the point where you can be counted and not be afraid—you're likely to be better adjusted, more confident, happier, more focused, more productive, and better off, even economically.

It doesn't mean that gay people are better than non-gay people. (One of the biggest obstacles to diversity of any kind is this nagging fear that "different" just might be "better.") But it does imply that, for lesbians and gay men, being out is better than being closeted.

Which brings us back to employment issues. All employers are likely to have gay and lesbian employees. So how do you want us? Honest, comfortable, and more likely to reach our potential?

How can you afford anything less?

Fear, Shame, and Flaunting, Heterosexual-Style

A gay-friendly company means, by definition, a workplace where openly gay and lesbian employees are comfortable. But it also implies that non-gay employees—certain to be the majority—are comfortable too.

The wide range of undertakings just described, and the groundswell of activity supporting them, reveals a significant shift in lesbian and gay consciousness. After many, many years, we are abandoning the way we see and portray ourselves as victims. That was a role mostly defined and imposed by non-gay people trying to seem sympathetic. We are now in the process of creating our own definitions, and that includes being strong and valuable assets to our employers or potential employers. The common cliché is that we are "empowering ourselves." And that shift, essential for us, can cause considerable discomfort among those who need to view us in the older way—with either hostility, condescension, or indifference. None of these are productive in today's workplace.

My belief is that the vast majority of non-gay Americans supports fairness and equality for gay men and lesbians—especially when those lesbians and gay men are family, friends, or respected coworkers. Yet most are unprepared for their part in the process involved: as we shed the burdens of fear and shame, the non-gay people around us will have to shed the mirror images of those irrationalities that they themselves hold.

Fear is paramount. Nobody likes to talk about it, but it's there. When Lotus Development introduced domestic-partner benefits for lesbian and gay employees in September 1991, the first publicly held company to do so, a surprisingly negative story in *The Wall Street Journal* sought to play up internal controversy. It quoted one employee, unnamed but described as "uncomfortable," as saying, "It will almost certainly over time make Lotus increasingly gay."

But the article doesn't identify what that means, or how it would be a problem.

Similarly, over lunch at a diversity conference in New York, the human resources director of a major footwear company confides to me that his company is having difficulty relocating (presumably non-gay) employees to its San Francisco office. He says, "People think San Francisco is too gay."

I can only contrast that with a story told to me by a lesbian colleague after a two-day business trip to San Francisco with a (non-gay) client to whom she was not out. On the plane home, he said to her, "Gee, for all its reputation, I didn't see a gay person the whole time we were there." Of course—as she had well noticed—whenever they had gone out for a meal and even at a few meetings, there had been lesbian and gay individuals or couples present. Not that much different from what you might find in Los Angeles or New York or any other business center.

It's not necessarily fair, but more than a few gay people get an ironic laugh from this sort of fear. It may be less likely today that you'd lose your job because you're gay (unless you're in the military), but you may still lose a promotion or your career. And it's still possible (in fact, because of backlash, even more likely today) to be beaten bloody by people who don't like you because you're gay, even in the streets of San Francisco or New York. When you're accustomed to dealing with fear based on experience, it's difficult to feel sympathy or fear based on myth. But both fears, like all fear, are based on uncertainty. Both are counterproductive and need to be addressed in an atmosphere of trust.

Shifting Shame

Shame, on the other hand, has undergone a profound shift that could be seen as a barometer of progress. Shame, according to social scientists, comes in two distinct varieties. One is "healthy" shame, that inner sense that controls how we act in a social context—it's the valve that implements our morals, our sense of what's right and what's wrong. This is the type of shame, according to stereotype, that gay men and lesbians don't have. It's what the uninformed draw on when they assume we don't know how to behave in a submarine bunk or in a client meeting.

The other shame, sometimes called "toxic" shame, is internalized self-hatred, something deeply programmed into you that tells you you are inherently bad. Without any kind of antidote, this poison can easily lead to depression, substance abuse, and other forms of self-destructive behavior. Gay men and lesbians are fed this programming in abundance by all types of social messages, by families, by religions.

The great joy of the lesbian and gay movement over recent decades has been developing the antidote against this poison. We are not *bad* simply because we were born with a different sexual orientation than most people. We can't change that; it's nothing to shame ourselves for. Instead, the challenge is separating toxic from healthy shame, learning how to work with that reality in the context of what's "right" and "wrong." Gay people can have a very strong sense of personal morality, simply because we've had to wrestle with issues more than most. Sometimes I think this is why we terrify certain moralistic religious or political leaders who try to suppress what we have to say.

That's where a significant shift has occurred in the ownership of shame, and it's exhibiting itself in the workplace. As lesbians and gay men struggle to shed the problems of self-hatred and to be happier, more productive humans, there are people who feel compelled to stop us. When their objections are based on religious belief, these deserve to be respected—as a regulator for themselves. When their objections are said to be based on morality, they have little to support them except tradition, always a helpful tool for any prejudice.

But here's an illustration of shifting shame. When the 3M Corporation (Minnesota Mining and Manufacturing) decided in the summer of 1992 to adopt a policy that prohibited discrimination on the basis of sexual orientation, it presented the news in its employee magazine, in the form of an interview with the director of human resources. The article was calm and thoughtful, explaining why the policy was adopted (employees had come forward with incidents of discrimination and harassment), how the policy was consistent with the company's revered tradition of human values (it just needed to be spelled out), whose responsibility the new policy was (everyone's), and where to call for advice and assistance. An admirable approach.

After the article ran, the magazine was deluged with letters as it had never seen before. For the next several issues, the letters page discussed nothing but this topic. As the editor told me, the mail was running about fifty-fifty, and she tried to show a fair representation. What appeared? Letters that applauded the new policy and some that took a neutral "let's see" attitude—some writers identified themselves as gay or not—all signed with locations and departments. Among the opposition, the letters ranged from careful arguments to the completely incomprehensible, but the majority of them were published unsigned.

How's that for a shift? Ten or twenty years ago, the situations would have been reversed—and the brave signature under a pro-gay stance probably would have been that of someone with impeccable heterosexual credentials. Sure, people might be cautious about taking a stance contrary to that of their employer. But that's at least a shallow form of healthy shame in operation. Bigotry is not socially acceptable anymore. (I don't pretend to know how much of this shifted shame is toxic, that is, internalized self-hatred—it happens to non-gay people, too. In extreme cases, this problem may deserve special attention.)

Who's Flaunting Now?

The new outlook of lesbians and gay men, combined with the realignments of fear and shame, underscores the importance of education to deal with issues of homophobia. An emotionally charged atmosphere of confrontation is an obvious obstacle to teamwork and productivity.

Ridding the workplace of institutionalized prejudice is essential, but it represents only the first steps of a larger process of change. If I may make an analogy, it's like stopping lynchings and eliminating Jim Crow laws and then thinking you've solved the problem of racism. Only now does it become possible to see the much larger and more subtle form of discrimination common even in supposedly sophisticated areas such as New York and San Francisco. It's the problem of the double standard— as in "I don't care if he's gay, as long as he doesn't flaunt it."

"Flaunting it" is one of those mysterious, undefined areas of offensiveness (to heterosexuals), along the lines of "incompatible with military service." What does it mean? If one of the goals of diversity is to establish comfortable boundaries for coexistence, isn't it necessary to define what the real concerns are?

Let's cut to the chase here: What non-gay men want is not to be sexually harassed on the job (or anywhere else). It's exactly the same thing everybody else wants, women (lesbian and not) and gay men included. That's a fair standard. The problem is that, for men, this is a relatively new phenomenon to be concerned with (women, lesbian and not, have a lot more experience coping with it) and for too many non-gay men, the mere proximity of an openly gay man is perceived as a threat. (Remember, gay people are not supposed to know how to behave.) Self-flattery aside, non-gay men would just rather not know. (Don't ask, don't tell.)

Thus, "flaunting" (applied to both lesbians and gay men, but more frequently to the men) can mean a simple statement of being gay. It can mean talking about your friends (when they're gay too) or where you went on vacation (especially if it's Fire Island or the like). It can mean talking about your home life (if you're in a relationship) or having a picture of your partner on your desk or (gasp) bringing that partner to a company function.

The irony, of course, is that non-gay people are constantly "flaunting" their heterosexuality. It happens when they talk about their friends (especially when matters of eligibility or sexual availability are involved), when they talk about their vacations (I love it when people talk about going to the "non-gay" parts of Fire Island), and most emphatically when they talk about their home life, put pictures of their spouses on their desks, and bring those spouses to company functions. But no one ever questions that.

Heterosexism is a clumsy but accurate term that means

"the assumption that everyone is heterosexual or ought to be." It's the prevailing attitude in our society, expressed with a lot of judgmental high-handedness. And it is constantly gnawing away at relations between non-gay people and their lesbian and gay colleagues. It breaks down trust, builds resentment, and feeds into problems such as sexism and racism by insisting that one person, by nature, is better than another.

How do we stop it? By putting aside myths and stereotypes and learning just who gay men and lesbians really are, and what we want.

Who Are We?

Nobody knows exactly how many lesbians and gay men there are, and that may always remain true. We're a minority that can't be counted. The studies of the Kinsey Institute of the 1940s and 1950s (which still seem to be the most scientifically reliable) estimated us at ten percent of the population. In more recent studies, French researchers settled on four percent, while the Battelle Institute in the United States (with questionable technique and motivation) is insisting on one percent. This last figure became the joke of the April 1993 March on Washington for lesbian and gay rights: Would all one percent (2.5 million) of us show up? Actually, not quite a million arrived—but there wasn't a gay man or lesbian there who couldn't think of at least five or ten others who stayed home. We know it's not all done with mirrors.

But the numbers game is misleading. Those who try to diminish the figures are simply trying to justify their own politics of denial. Those who try to inflate our numbers are dealing in a lot of speculation. We already know that at least some politicians take us seriously as a voting bloc. We know that we've earned respect as consumers, at least in some markets. We know we have an impact on all of society, in thinking, culture, education, style, and the expansion of human rights. None of these significant things depend very much on how many of us there are. They are the results of what we *do*.

As people who have been allowed to uncover our own history only in the past few decades, we're sometimes startled to find among our own number so many women and men who changed the world. (I won't include the list here; as with all of recorded history, it's heavily weighted with men.) Simultaneously, we can look around in our daily lives and see that we hold every position in society imaginable. We are teachers, doctors, architects, lawyers, researchers, assembly line workers, shopkeepers, mail carriers, soldiers, sailors, members of Congress, clerks, telephone installers, computer programmers, public relations executives, landscapers, bartenders, priests, CEOs, accountants, truck drivers and the people who unload the trucks, workers and managers of every stripe. When it comes to our jobs and careers, no stereotype works.

Of course, half of us are women, and we include in our numbers members of every age, racial, ethnic, religious, or other group. In the workplace, that's not always so apparent. What the workplace tends to see, as society tends to see, is an outspoken group of gay white men. Some self-criticism is deserved here: yes, there is sexism and racism in our community—not surprising, considering where we come from. But I know of few other groups that work as hard for diversity outreach within our own ranks. And I know of few other groups of white men who are as willing to take the front ranks—at the risk of their own social advantages—for the common good. There are lessons here for every organization's diversity efforts.

Increasingly, lesbians (albeit predominantly white lesbians) are taking the leadership roles they deserve. I think this has much to do with changes within the lesbian and gay community, within society's attitude toward women (especially in the workplace), and within the lesbians themselves. It has been a powerful source of new vitality. However, issues of race have not yet broken through. Gay and lesbian people of color point to concerns about having two strikes against them (three for women). These are justifiable concerns. Attitudes in the traditional workplace are sexist, racist, and homophobic. But it also betrays the complexity of attitudes within different racial groups toward sexual orientation. These need to be addressed. I'm not sure whether workplace diversity programs are prepared to deal with this—even when they deal with lesbian and gay issues, there seems to be a prevailing white-bread context. But it's essential at least to be aware. We may all share goals as gay men and lesbians, but each of us has additional challenges as well.

What else does an employer need to know about us? What do we know about ourselves? We've already looked at what market research is saying about our income, education, and consumer habits. Related research has found that we work in all fields. (We do have a strong presence in the fields of education and health care; these professions, ironically, often necessitate closeted behavior.) Others are trying to analyze our behavior in other ways. Per Larson, for example, a financial adviser, is finding interesting patterns in the financial lives of gay men and lesbians that differ markedly from the typical heterosexual-married model. Someday I'd like to see a study of entrepreneurship among lesbians and gay men. We know there's a lot of it out there. Is it because of bad experiences we've had in past workplaces? Because we're more willing to take risks? Because we just had a better idea? All these theories have implications for the business world.

My friend Jay Lucas, a Philadelphia-based diversity trainer, has done a pioneering study on the behavior of lesbians and gay men in the workplace, much of it published in the book he coauthored with James Woods, *The Corporate Closet*. Based on extensive interviews, he finds three basic types of behavior: "hiding" or "counterfeiting," which involves inventing a fictional life to cover the reality; "avoiding," which requires continuous self-editing and half-truths; and "integrating," in which a gay or lesbian employee comes out and is able to successfully manage the consequences. "Avoiding" seems to be the most common today; nearly all of us have done it at some point in our lives. Non-gay people seemed to have learned the strategy well too. One gay man recently told me how he was "figured out" by his coworkers. They said, "You had to be gay. We didn't know anything about you. You'd say you went to the movies, but you'd never say with whom." So much for the secrets we think we keep.

Generation Gaps

From my own observations, there is much to be considered about the connection between behavior and age or, more specifically, rapidly evolving generations. There are currently three distinct generations of lesbians and gay men in the workplace. Sometimes our attitudes can diverge sharply along those lines, often more so than by gender, race, or other attributes. That's how quickly we're changing.

The boundaries of these generations are marked more by attitudes and collective experience than by precise age—which has variations based on region, upbringing, life influences, current situation, and so on—and there are exceptions in every classification. But we might define the eldest group as roughly over fifty. These men and women came of age soon after World War II. (Korea was their war, and so was the one called Cold.) Their world was more than big-finned cars; it included McCarthyism, the bomb, and all the stifling conformity that seems so quaint on TV reruns. They were adults at the time of the watershed Stonewall Rebellion and its message of liberation—indeed, some of them *were* Stonewall. The vast majority took the advice of the Mattachine Society during the riots: stay home, stay calm, everything will be all right. And most remain that way today.

Younger groups are often harsh in their judgment,

considering them "closet cases," because they are indeed among those who raised "hiding" behavior to a fine art, most especially in the workplace. They had good reason to be afraid in an era of witch hunts, imprisonment, and disgrace.

Yet it was this same group who were the founding pioneers of the modern gay and lesbian community. It was they who created the first organizations, neighborhoods, and places to gather and network that remain the focal point of lesbian and gay life. They just did it very quietly. Their primary challenge was to overcome the isolation that every gay man and lesbian grows up with, to bring us together for mutual support. They accomplished that, but fearfully. And not only do they still carry much of that fear inside of them, but they passed it on as a legacy to the next generation.

The post-Stonewall generation, aged roughly thirty to fifty, is easily identified as the Baby Boomers. There are many things I could say about us (for I am squarely in the middle of that cohort), but what is probably most important is that, steeped in the activism of the times—civil rights, women's rights, the Vietnam War, and, of course, the "sexual revolution"—we passionately picked up the (double-edged) sword of liberation. We knew *our* challenge was to overcome fear. We did it by coming out as far as each dared: family, friends, but almost never on the job. Our focal point was the law; as it had for others, the law would protect us. Or so we thought. As we educated ourselves and others and fought our way toward legal protection, we were processing out our fears.

But, of course, the post-Stonewall generation very

suddenly took on a different distinction: we are the AIDS generation, the core of a devastating epidemic. There was nothing that tested our fears more than AIDS could. First, in silent terror, we watched in denial as an unknown disease decimated our numbers, ripped out our hearts, and destroyed the lives we thought we had comfortably—and safely—established. Then realizing that no one was going to help us unless we did it for ourselves, we exploded with a collective emotion more potent than fear: anger. Anger became the energy source that powered us to make change, not only on the AIDS front but, in the process, on all the issues of lesbian and gay rights. Anger brought us to confront, head-on, our governments, our churches, the media, the health-care system, any institution—even if it meant coming out on the job. Who was afraid of that anymore? There was much worse.

The more conservative of our number have sat out the activism, but they understand the emotion. They are just processing it at a more gradual speed. Most found creative and productive ways of channeling our anger, but there is no underestimating its power, now and, I suspect, for the rest of our lives. The horrors of what we have seen—still denied by much of the non-gay world—have infused us with an urgency expressed in terms such as "Cure AIDS Now!" But anger has also given us an outlook that says, "Never again." Anger broke down, and is still breaking down, the divisions in our lives—certainly those that now seem so much less significant, such as separating the personal from the professional. And anger is certainly, whether we intended to or not, the legacy we handed to the next generation.

For gay men and lesbians under thirty, anger is a given—sometimes to the surprise of those of us who feel like fossils at forty. We have already ceded much of the leadership of our movement to their energy. What they—Generation X, is it?—will do with it is still uncertain. But they are sharp, very serious, cynical, and they suffer no fools. They are clever—who else could have made being gay, well, so *stylish?* Of course, they seem to be fearless. Coming out is something they do early, often, and everywhere. Bless them. The phenomenon seems especially intense on college campuses today. And guess who's coming to your workplace?

When generations evolve so rapidly, they can collide. If the activism of my generation embarrassed or seemed to threaten the one before us, one can be sure the attitudes of the youngest absolutely terrify them. Not surprisingly, the differences show themselves in the workplace, where age has a close correlation to the ranking of upper, middle, and entry-level personnel. One of the most common complaints I hear from openly lesbian and gay employees—privately—is, "There is this closet case upstairs who is making my life very difficult."

Strong emotions are involved here—anger and fear—as well as different outlooks on what's wrong, or what can or should be done. In addition, we find ourselves at different stages of life: some looking forward to retirement, others trying to make the most of the peak of their careers, still others ambitiously mapping out their futures. But the generational influences feed upward too: a look at those younger reminds you of the things you never tried, but now just might. More than ever before, we are all pushing limits we never before dared. And while our numbers may seem small, we are already exerting an impact on society, the marketplace, and the workplace.

And how does the majority react to that? When our contribution is given at the cost of our identities, it is gratefully received, even celebrated. When it bears our name, it is often resisted. Much of this resistance is, not coincidentally, generational. Those over fifty who do not know us among their closeted peers react the most sharply. Those under thirty, who do know us, welcome the added value. Time is on our side. But can we waste time?

The experience of our own movement has shown that any problems with difference within the lesbian and gay community—age, gender, race, class, beliefs, and on and on—are surmounted most effectively when we recognize the shared purpose and mutual benefit in working together. Since we live with the struggle daily, we gay men and lesbians need to keep reminding ourselves. But any organization attempting to deal with the challenge of diversity might do well to learn from our experience. If there's an ability to ask.

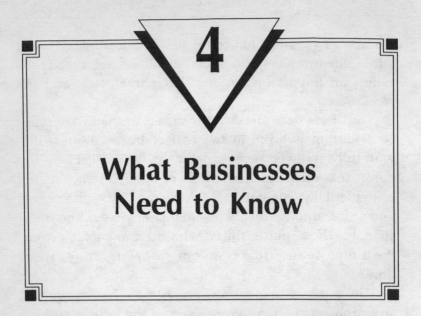

What Businesses
Need to Know

Sometimes I have to remind myself: business is essentially amoral. Businesses don't do something because it's "the right thing to do." *Individuals* do that. And sometimes an individual is influential enough to steer an entire business in a philosophical direction. But businesses act and react simply to meet the needs of business.

With changes in the law, employee relations, recruitment, investor relations, and marketing, there are plenty of solid, economic reasons for businesses to become gay-friendly. But how do they show it? How do they prove it?

Some companies confuse themselves with individuals, thinking that they're gay-friendly because they have been tolerant of openly gay and lesbian employees. What's really going on is that certain intelligent and responsive managers have made the choice to do the right thing. Individuals even in the most homophobic companies can do that.

When the *Los Angeles Times* asked me in the spring of 1993 to provide them with a list of "tips" for "how managers should behave when a worker comes out," this is what I came up with:

Show support. Say "I don't discriminate and I won't permit harassment or prejudiced behavior in my department." Hopefully the company already has such a policy. Add that the employee can talk to you if any harassment occurs.

Live up to what you said. If there is a harassment situation, such as jokes or nasty graffiti, intervene and make a statement. Say, "We don't tolerate that kind of behavior here." People can believe what they want to believe, but they shouldn't act out that behavior if it damages another employee.

Let the employee chart the course. Coming out is a critical and vulnerable point in a person's development, and everyone does it differently. Don't pry. Don't lecture. Be businesslike. Just offer a safe space.

Put yourself in the other person's position. Think about how you'd feel dealing with nasty jokes, stereotyping, or having your family left out of company-sponsored family events. How would you want to change company policies if you were in that person's shoes?

That's a good start for a gay-friendly manager, or even a management philosophy, but it doesn't make a gay-friendly company. A company has to take a serious look at its prevailing culture and implement changes organization-wide.

Every workplace is different and has different circumstances to deal with. But there has to be a basic standard that describes what lesbian and gay employees need and want. Around 1990, after discussions with managers and with gay and lesbian employees, I put together a list of "Ten Suggestions for a More Honest and Inclusive Workplace." It dealt with specific issues such as prejudiced personnel forms, double-standard attitudes toward lesbian and gay visibility, and the importance of support in the face of criticism. People seemed to respond well to it, given the number of times I heard it recited or had it given to me as a handout in other people's workshops.

But I soon realized that the list could be refined to three basic and easily understood points, which I sometimes see as progressive steps toward creating a gay-friendly company. They cover non-discrimination policy, education and training efforts, and equal benefits and compensation.

Non-Discrimination Policy

It is absolutely essential for employers to have a written statement that explicitly states the organization does not discriminate on the basis of sexual orientation.

This can be accomplished simply by writing the words "sexual orientation" into an existing Equal Employment Opportunity (EEO) statement, which likely includes race, gender, age, religion, national origin, disability, and/or veteran status. The statement may be short and to the point or may elaborate that this means hiring, training, promoting, working conditions, and so on. It may also explain why the company thinks this is important, who is responsible for carrying it out, or even the penalties incurred for violation. Fine. What matters is that it is written.

Why is that so important? Written policy is the foundation for all the rules and guiding principles that govern a workplace. It's the basis for all corporate culture. Written policy is stronger than tradition, custom, or hearsay, because anyone with a question can look it up and refer back to it when needed. Without a written policy, how else will lesbian and gay employees *know* they won't be discriminated against? And how else will managers know that anti-gay behavior is not permitted here? (There are enough messages that say it's permitted elsewhere.)

Unfortunately, most companies miss this point or choose to miss this point. For a survey on gay and lesbian workplace issues conducted by the Society for Human Resource Management in early 1993, I helped prepare the questionnaire and included what was admittedly a trick question. The very first question asked companies if they prohibited discrimination on the basis of sexual orientation. Nearly two-thirds of the respondents said "Yes." The next question asked if they had a *written* policy saying the same. Only about one-half of those who said "Yes" to the first question could say "Yes" to the second. I mean, how is anyone supposed to know?

If that survey is any indicator, only one in three

American companies offers any written reassurance at all to gay and lesbian employees.

Some companies, when asked, actually try to claim some degree of protection because their EEO statement includes the phrase "and any other form of discrimination prohibited by local law." This is almost laughable: what company is going to admit to violating the law? But it poses more serious questions, especially when a company has more than one location. Does that mean a lesbian or gay employee is "safe" working in an office in Chicago, which has protective legislation, but not in a meeting at a facility in suburban Arlington Heights, which doesn't? And what happens in a transfer? None of this is very reassuring. Nor does it say that the company places any value on its gay and lesbian employees.

Policy must be written, specific, and company-wide if it's to have any meaning at all. If it's to be effective, there's one more requirement: it has to be communicated.

How many employees actually read through their personnel manuals? Not many. I often ask gay men and lesbians, in both professional and social settings, whether their employers have non-discrimination policies for sexual orientation. Many don't know. Many of these people are managers themselves. Sometimes I get calls back to tell me they checked policy and, yes, it's there. Then, reflecting on their own stress from dealing with a homophobic environment, they add, "But you'd never know it."

What good is a policy if it's kept a secret? Most of the time, the secrecy is not deliberate. For heaven's sake, people are busy *working* around here. But the problem is, unless a policy is somehow reiterated in a routine way, it gets forgotten—if anyone knew it in the first place. Any kind of management training is a logical place to put a reminder. Or the employee publication. Or electronic mail. Some enterprising diversity and human resources departments use current events as a hook for pointing out internal policy. No, it doesn't have to mean getting embroiled in controversy. But, during the highly publicized Anita Hill–Clarence Thomas hearings in Congress, AT&T made the connection and used its E-mail to define the company's own stand on sexual harassment. Admirable. Who did the equivalent during the gays-in-the-military fiasco?

Enforcement is the real test for policy, of course. Large companies tend to develop a lot of policies, some of which are generally recognized as downright zany. What's to say that the non-discrimination policy isn't just another bunch of those words? Especially in the case of anti-gay discrimination? With any kind of policy, the violation that goes ignored can soon become commonplace, part of the corporate culture. It might mean filling out some redundant forms. Or it might be petty theft. Or misleading customers. Policies worth having are worth enforcing. Otherwise, well, who cares?

Discrimination policies are always problematic. First they require an employee courageous enough to stand up and claim discrimination. Then there's the difficult problem of proving it. When it concerns women and most minorities, federal law comes into play. (Lesbians and gay men don't have that assistance, only the protection of certain local laws.) But companies that find themselves in legal imbroglios usually have a systemic problem that could've been addressed long before.

Reports of anti-gay discrimination have to be taken seriously, or incidents will become rampant (if they aren't already). A lot of information will be passed in gossip or witnessed in graffiti and offhand comments. The importance of these shouldn't be overlooked. Typically, when it comes to anti-gay discrimination, the worse the situation is, the less likely it is that complaints are being filed. Lesbian and gay employees are too afraid. And typically, when these situations break open, they can do so explosively, with an anger-driven coming-out, the loss of a valued employee, the possibility of a lawsuit, and a lot of unflattering publicity.

Ultimately, the communication and enforcement of policy depends on the support of top management. The best diversity programs anywhere are those endorsed publicly and frequently by the CEO. More than just a bunch of words, the CEO sets the example. If that person makes it clear that fag or dyke jokes aren't welcome here or shakes hands with an openly gay employee who has done a good job or welcomes at a company's "family" event an employee's same-sex partner—well, everyone else will notice. And it's remarkable how quickly attitudes and actions fall into line with policy.

Education and Training

Why should a company do any education at all, let alone on gay and lesbian issues? (There's no "Lesbian and Gay Lives" category on *Jeopardy!* If there were, we wouldn't need this book.)

It seems that business gets stuck doing a lot of the things that society in general doesn't do very well, if at all. (I'm avoiding the temptation to cite any classic Republican rhetoric.) There doesn't seem to be much question that when employees need to know a new software system the company trains them. To a certain extent, this is still true for basic computer literacy. On an even more elementary level, when a company is faced with a talent pool that is increasingly illiterate—here I mean reading, writing, and 'rithmetic—employers have a choice: do the remedial teaching themselves, work with the schools to solve a worsening problem, or ignore the situation until it catches up with them.

Companies do diversity training mainly because of the miserably low level of human-relations education in our society. Even decent people make offensive mistakes in gender and race relations. It's easy to do when you have little experience with people different from yourself. Ignorance is the problem, so companies make a diversity investment to encourage harmony, boost morale, and gain productivity.

The same is true with gay and lesbian issues, only more so. Most adults in the workforce today have little or no access to information about lesbians and gay men— unless a friend or family member happens to be one. Until barely a decade ago, there was a total blackout of information about us: at home, on TV, in the movies, in the papers, in the library, in school, in church—what you did hear was invariably *bad* and far from a balanced picture. (Apparently, the philosophy was—and still is for many—that if people, especially children, don't hear about us, they won't become us. Rest assured, the approach didn't work for me or any other gay person I've ever met.)

Recent attempts to fill that vacuum have been mixed. Yes, we do get better coverage in most major newspapers today, and sometimes the reporting is even balanced. There are thousands of books available on all sorts of aspects of gay and lesbian lives, but you'll be hard-pressed to find them in your average suburban mall bookstore. Librarians are wary; these days they still have to defend *The Catcher in the Rye*. Churches are struggling. Television has learned to treat us as news, but bigots howl when a fuller story is attempted on the networks— they threaten the sponsors. The major Hollywood studios rarely produce a gay or lesbian character who isn't evil, pathetic, or the queer equivalent of a character from *Amos 'n' Andy*—but they're promising. (It's interesting to note that whatever changes are occurring in these industries result mainly from lesbian and gay employees in them standing up and demanding better.)

Most schools below college level maintain the informational blackout. The controversy in New York over the Rainbow Curriculum, in which the barest mention is made that some loving families have gay members too and that ought to be respected, was presented as "teaching sodomy to first-graders." The few enlightened parents who speak matter-of-factly to their children about lesbian and gay life—generally in the context of family and friends—are considered peculiar. (As two friends have reported back to me, when their kindergartner tells a story in school about her Uncle Ed's boyfriend, or about her godmother who is "married to another lady," it merits a call home from a concerned teacher.)

So it shouldn't be a surprise to find that many, or most, of the non-gay workforce have complete ignorance of lesbians and gay men. That's not just a scenario for offensive mistakes. It means a sizable group of people who are terrified of those whom they see as evil, a danger to children, the source of AIDS, and other far-fetched ideas. In that way they can justify avoidance, harassment, and malicious gossip as well as firing, not hiring, and not promoting. Until they learn better.

What's a company to do? Take hold of the problem by filling the gap. Teach. There are three ways of doing it: by example, through diversity training, and by encouraging gay and lesbian employees to do it themselves.

Education by example is fairly simple; it follows pretty much the same lines recommended above for a CEO and for a manager trying to be supportive of an employee who has come out: Emphasize that there is no discrimination in this workplace—publicly. Back up your words—publicly. Make a special effort to reach out to lesbian and gay employees—we're not talking about special treatment here, just words and gestures to fill the silence that has caused so much fear and anxiety. This isn't about "taking sides" either; all you're trying to do is make sure all your employees are comfortable and able to work together. Listen. Show yourself open to talking about concerns of both gay and non-gay employees. You can do it in your own personal business style: formally or informally, in memos or in person, whatever. You might be pleasantly surprised by what you learn about your workforce, and most of them will certainly respect you for your accessibility and responsiveness.

Education by example is an ideal approach for the smaller company unable to take on a formal diversity program. (What's suggested for lesbian and gay employees should already be in place for women, other minorities, and anyone else who might be different—maybe even non-gay white men. In gay-owned businesses and in some AIDS service organizations, the challenge often is how to accommodate heterosexual employees.) Smaller organizations, after all, tend to be much more strongly stamped with the personalities of their leadership. That puts a bit more of a burden on the top to do some introspection. Just what are your own personal beliefs and prejudices? Can they interfere with the success of your business? Do you let them? The big boss should expect all managers and supervisors to follow suit. Honesty and consistency in an organization can have a remarkable effect.

Formal diversity programs continue to be the rage at larger companies, and even midsize ones. A program basically requires a plan, experienced diversity trainers (in-house ones or consultants), and the commitment of management to make it work. If the programs really foster better understanding among people who are different from one another, then they are a real benefit to business and society as a whole.

Unfortunately, the great majority of diversity programs still don't include even a minimal reference to gay and lesbian concerns. Perhaps there are some legitimate excuses for this. Diversity training requires a certain degree of delicacy in trust-building, and maybe the topic of sexual orientation is perceived as too explosive. But how much of that is just pandering to phobia, as in homophobia? I'm still inclined to say that it's unhealthy to be saying, even if unintentionally, "It's okay to be different, but not in *that* way."

One of the great disappointments I've had in putting together this book is not being able to include some fine companies with well-known and (otherwise) excellent diversity programs. One of these is Motorola.

During a diversity conference in Chicago in September 1992, I had the pleasure of meeting the chief architect of Motorola's diversity program. She's sharp, insightful, and deliciously funny, and between our respective presentations we had a chance to chat in the smoking lounge. Mostly, we talked personal stuff about interracial relationships (we were both in interracial marriages—although I'm not sure she would have allowed me that term). Finally, I asked her when Motorola would begin to include lesbian and gay issues in its much admired diversity program. She hesitated, then said, "Not yet." More than a year later, at this writing, it still hasn't happened. (Discussions, I'm told, started in 1994.)

If not now, when?

I happen to believe that resolving issues of gender and race is of paramount importance in improving the American workplace, and that you can't begin to address gay and lesbian issues until after you've begun looking at those. At the same time, all prejudices are interconnected—they're all about one group trying to assert superiority over another. There's a particularly striking parallel between racism and heterosexism, where the epithets are used to make sure you're demoted on the totem pole, where the minority is forced to live according to the definitions of the majority, and where the majority hasn't a clue about what the minority really thinks or feels.

Homophobia also has exceptionally close ties to sexism. This topic is worth several volumes in itself, but we might sum it up by saying that homosexuality is frequently seen (especially by those most afraid of it) as a blurring of the rigidly defined gender roles our society has come to depend on and which, not accidentally, are a convenient way to justify discrimination against women. One of the most distasteful (yet common) questions gay men and lesbians get asked by friends and colleagues is, "Who plays the man, and who's the woman?" Aside from the fact that it's none of their business and that it shows a real lack of imagination in terms of sexual practices, the question reveals the genuine anxiety many people have about equality of the genders. They need a clear definition and separation.

In the workplace, women know how this translates. But here's an illustration from the homophobia side. A lesbian friend of mine, then an executive at a Big Six accounting firm (but closeted on the job), told me this story only a few years ago. A male temporary was hired to help out in the secretarial pool. The (male) partner in charge of the area noticed this and demanded the temp's firing. The reason? "I won't have any fags working in my office." No one had any idea what the temp's sexual orientation actually was, but he was let go on some other excuse. The fact that he was a man in what was traditionally a woman's job was threatening enough to the partner. My friend witnessed this (yes, it was illegal in the city where it happened; no, no one did a thing about it). She could see exactly where she stood, as a woman and as a lesbian. She immediately began looking for another job.

Add to the interrelationships among homophobia, sexism, and racism the facts that half of the gay population are women, that we are represented in equal proportion in every race, and are included in every other classification, plus that each of us has a certain set of problematic circumstances to deal with in our respective, overlapping groups—and you get the beginnings of a very interesting matrix. But perhaps that's what scares some people off: the complexity of human relationships.

Diversity programs, caught in a mind-set from affirmative action, still deal with employees as members of groups. That may cause problems down the line, but, I suppose, at an elementary level it's the approach we have to take just to get people to learn about one another.

The first thing a diversity program has to establish is facts. This is the only way to supplant myths and misunderstandings. Then it has to move toward understanding, and this includes feelings: if you grow up this way and have these types of experiences, you might act or react in a certain way, have certain motivations and certain sensitivities. Others need to be aware of these, and perhaps alter their own behavior, in the interests of working more effectively together. Ultimately, a diversity program should impart the idea that being different (and in some way, who isn't?) is not only okay—there's the "victim" pitfall—but a potentially valuable asset in the effort to achieve shared goals. Sure, it's a tall order.

Getting the facts and even some of the feelings across could be accomplished with lectures and readings. But that's a bit on the dry side. Trainers have found it a great deal more effective (when blessed with manageable-size groups at training sessions) to use exercises (less respectfully called games) that encourage more learning through a process of self-discovery. There are many of these, and new ones are being invented all the time. Many of them are useful for exploring all types of differences, but some seem to work best when dealing with issues unique to sexual orientation.

Here's a simple one for dealing with questions about whether it's "appropriate" for lesbians and gay men to come out, or whether they should stay closeted (this is where "flaunting" meets the "personal vs. professional" dilemma). Participants are given a plain sheet of paper. They are asked to think about someone whom they work with on a frequent basis and with whom they think they have a good working relationship. Then they are asked to write down everything *personal* they know about this coworker.

Participants are often astonished by how much they do know. Not just marital status, they'll know the spouse's name—whom they've probably met—maybe even the condition of the marriage. Not just that the co-worker took a vacation, but also the destination, who went along, and what kind of time was had by all. They'll know about kids (or lack of same), friends, community involvement, hobbies, hangouts, political views, and so on. None of this information is essential to doing the job, but it seems to be an important part of building relationships, trust, and comfort among colleagues. Yet so much of this information is just what gay men and lesbians can't talk about unless they're out—or lying.

Similarly, there are endless variations on the "pronoun roulette" game that closeted gay people play all the time. One scenario: You woke up this morning. You were not alone. Now describe everything that happened to you between that moment and the time you left for work—but you can't use any third-person pronouns (the gender-specific *he* or *she*).

For more direct role-playing, it's useful for a non-gay person to be given the following directives: You're gay. You don't want anyone to know. You're in a committed relationship. The two of you have just come back from a week's vacation at a famous gay resort. You've had a wonderful time. You feel great. You look great. A colleague walks up to you and asks, "Gee, where were you?" What do you answer?

Or take the same circumstances and imagine that your partner is very ill. You're worried. You're distracted. The situation is demanding a lot of your time. People ask what's wrong. What do you say? (I have a fantasy that someday, when honesty is allowed to prevail in our society, this would be the sort of question for a game show. Lesbian and Gay Lives for $100, please.)

For groups that are themselves diverse, I think it's

important to emphasize the diversity within the lesbian and gay community, which too many people perceive as overwhelmingly white and male. (Like the population as a whole, white males are in the minority.) For this I came up with "Name That Queer." (Please don't be offended by the term: I use it because it's gender-free and fast to say in a beat-the-clock atmosphere.) I select random members of the group and give each ten seconds to name a famous, well, queer. (No outing here; the person has to be dead or self-stated.) Invariably, the first five are white men. So I get more specific. Lesbian. African-American. Asian. Hispanic. Lesbian Hispanic. And so on. Sometimes I give hints, but people (gay or not) who know their own group's heritage can usually come up with an answer and get an opportunity to explain to the others—so everybody learns. (Lesbian and Gay Lives for $300, please.)

The double standard of heterosexism is a tough one for non-gay people to understand. But an exercise called the reverse questionnaire offers some illumination. You divide groups into pairs and make one person in each pair the "designated heterosexual." The other then proceeds to ask a series of questions. Here's a sample:

- What do you think caused your heterosexuality?
- When and how did you decide you were heterosexual?
- Is it possible that heterosexuality is just a phase you may grow out of?
- Why do heterosexuals feel compelled to seduce others into their lifestyle?

- If you've never slept with a person of the same sex, is it possible that all you need is a good same-sex lover?
- Why do you insist on flaunting your heterosexuality? Why can't you just be who you are and keep quiet about it?
- The vast majority (over ninety-six percent) of child molesters are heterosexual. Do you consider it safe to expose your children to heterosexual teachers?
- With all the social support marriage receives, the divorce rate is still fifty percent. Why are there so few stable relationships among heterosexuals?
- Considering the menace of hunger and overpopulation, can the human race survive if everyone were heterosexual like yourself?
- The group with the fastest growing number of AIDS cases is heterosexual. Shouldn't we prohibit sex between heterosexuals?

And so on. Obviously, all of these exercises have the potential to touch on some really sensitive points in people's psyches, and that has to be respected. So I'm not suggesting a do-it-yourself approach. They should be implemented by an experienced facilitator, in an atmosphere of trust, without the threat of confrontation, and—hopefully—with some sense of humor.

That last item on the reverse questionnaire should bring up issues of AIDS and HIV education, which I haven't dealt with at all. Let me explain. Although AIDS is commonly used as an excuse to discriminate against gay men (who are still, within the general U.S. population, the largest single group infected or affected) *and* lesbians (who are practically the smallest infected group), it would be a mistake to reinforce thinking of AIDS as a gay issue. These days, nearly everyone can be at risk for AIDS (especially those who think they're not), and businesses need to address AIDS and HIV as universal health and prevention issues. Excellent programs and materials are available through organizations such as the National Leadership Coalition on AIDS, which specializes in AIDS education and issues in the workplace. Of course, because of the overlap in fear and prejudice, a good program in AIDS and HIV education makes an ideal precursor to programs dealing specifically with gay and lesbian concerns.

Whether the educational approach is by example or through diversity training, its impact is increased exponentially with personal testimony. That is, by having an open and visible lesbian or gay employee to make political abstractions into tangible reality. At least one. (If you can't get one to stand up, your organization probably has a lot of pain and fear to make up for.)

When teaching by example, how you interact with the gay or lesbian employee says it all. Of course, that puts a lot of pressure on the gay or lesbian employee (being the *only* one is always a burden), so you're relying on how up-front that employee wants to be. We're not talking about "flaunting" here, or being "neutral" (in the sense of ignoring the difference when it shouldn't be ignored), or tokenism—it's a careful judgment call to avoid all three. But is the employee comfortable being out? Is he or she able to talk about sexual orientation issues when they arise? Is homophobic behavior being dealt with expediently? Perhaps most important, is his or her career moving on a track commensurate with his or her talent? Gradually, if this is working, other lesbian or gay employees will feel confident enough to come out too. And you'll notice the difference.

In diversity training, personal testimony might be conveyed by a gay or lesbian trainer, guest speaker, or even through videotape, but nothing works like having one of the group stand up to say, "That's me you're talking about, and here's how it really is . . ." This can happen randomly in groups or, better, it can be programmed by having a lesbian or gay employee join the group to talk. But this assumes that enough employees are out and locatable—and that probably means networked.

Gay men and lesbians in any predominantly non-gay group tend to find one another, either by actually meeting in some gay venue or by the somewhat mysterious but very real phenomenon known as "gay radar," our uncanny ability to recognize one another—which is not the same as sexual attraction. At work, anyone who is severely closeted will run away from these situations screaming. However, those willing to trust their fellows create an informal network, clandestine if necessary, for friendship and moral support in the face of adversity. As purges in the military have often proven, these groups can be tightly knit and protective of one another's identity.

In friendlier workplaces, or in really bad ones where a brave leader arises, these groups often become visible and more formally organized. This is especially true in larger organizations. They'll have official meetings.

They'll adopt a name. They'll look at shared problems, and they'll develop a plan. And then they may choose to go public. Sometimes they'll even split into two groups, one for socializing and support, another for advocacy within the company.

The challenge for any organization at this point is to decide whether or not to ignore the group (as is often the case with companies that are terrified of union organizing) or to recognize the group and legitimize it. Obviously, a gay-friendly company does the latter.

By doing so, the company gets an opportunity to work with an enormous amount of energy that's channeled toward constructive goals. The company wins a lot of employee goodwill in this way (gay and not). It gets a few representatives (instead of a disgruntled crowd) who can articulate what problems exist and help strategize solutions. And it will acquire a dynamic team of teachers and trainers who with enthusiasm will design and implement a program to encourage understanding, tolerance, and ways in which we can all work together more effectively. It's the best approach to lesbian and gay issues any diversity program could ask for. (Lesbian and Gay Lives for $500, please.)

Some companies subsidize these efforts. (The standard I look for is whether all employee affinity groups—women, African-Americans, veterans, disabled, and the rest—are treated and funded equally.) Some companies don't but still encourage activity. What the group can do might include awareness programs, written materials, workplace events and celebrations, community volunteer work as a group, or participating in major lesbian and gay conclaves (like the annual Gay Pride festivities) under the company's banner. Unfortunately, even gay-friendly companies don't always permit the last one or two, even though they carry enormous public relations value within the lesbian and gay community. They're scared. And sadly, that's the *real* corporate closet.

It's still not unusual to hear a company explain, when refusing to recognize a gay and lesbian employee group or to allow them to identify themselves under the corporate name, that the company is not in the business of "endorsing a lifestyle"—or something to that effect. Let's forget about the "lifestyle" concept here—repeat, there is no such thing as "a gay lifestyle"—and just look at the "endorsement" mistake. Recognizing and acknowledging reality is not an endorsement. That confusion is a critical concern to people whose deepest scars are the product of silence. And it reflects back to one of the core issues in diversity education: changing behavior vs. changing belief.

All people are entitled to believe what they believe. This is one of the most glorious tenets of the American way of life. However, there's a corollary: you can't always act out what you believe, especially when it violates the beliefs and rights of a fellow citizen. Diversity education has to be strictly based on both the rule and the corollary. Belief should be inviolate, but behavior can and should be regulated in the workplace. There are plenty of people with strong beliefs about race, ethnicity, the role of women, disabilities, even about marital status, height and weight, or an occasional drink. But these beliefs can't (by law) or shouldn't (by fairness) be allowed to influence business behavior, through prejudice in hiring, promotion, or everyday treatment. Diversity education might have an effect on these beliefs, just as building a relationship with someone different from yourself might. But the bottom line is about establishing standards of behavior that rise above prejudice and create a welcoming atmosphere that makes the most of all human potential. And, no matter what some people may believe, lesbians and gay men want to be part of that process—as equals.

Education is no quick fix. It's a long-term process that can take years to assess. But companies can take steps to speed up the impact of efforts to encourage diversity. It's not, as in affirmative action, by counting heads—which only begins to reveal more subtle problems of discrimination, such as the "glass ceiling." Companies can show they are responsive to the needs of their increasingly pluralistic workforce. They can make diversity programs mandatory for all employees or at least all managers. They can use their influence to encourage positive change among their vendors and suppliers. They can look at all their own policies and stances, to see where inequality or a double standard exists. One small thing they can do, which may have the greatest impact of all, is to add to the routine assessment of each and every employee's performance the question: "How well does the employee work with those who are different from him/herself?"

Benefits and Compensation

A 1990 study by the U.S. Chamber of Commerce reported that the average American worker receives about forty percent of his or her total compensation in the form of benefits. This figure struck a nerve among lesbians and gay men who were beginning to look beyond issues of safety and acceptance in the workplace. We were looking at equality. Was it true that those of us who get no support or recognition for our families were actually getting paid forty percent less than our married colleagues?

Actually, no. A closer look at the figures showed that about three-fourths of the value of those benefits (including paid time off, life insurance, retirement and savings funds, unemployment and workers' compensation) applied directly to the individual employee. That left about ten percent for health benefits, of which half were specifically for spouses and dependents. So the discount was more like five percent. Unfair, yes. But that's not what really hurts.

Despite all the negative stereotyping we grow up with and all the attacks we hear that debase our relationships—or maybe because of them—we know that falling in love, building a relationship, and keeping a family together are among the finest things we can do with our lives. Perhaps more than those who get them more easily, we value our partnerships and families.

It didn't seem fair that those of us who had relationships that looked like a marriage, felt like a marriage, talked like a marriage, worked like a marriage, cost like a marriage, gave emotional support like a marriage, and involved stress like a marriage could be told we didn't have a marriage because we're denied a piece of paper that says we're married. That's long been true. But to realize that we're being paid five percent less than our colleagues whose lives are almost identical to our own, except that they have access to a certificate—well, that's just plain galling.

"Domestic-partner benefits" have rapidly become a central issue for lesbian and gay workers. As far as individual benefits are concerned, we usually don't experience discrimination, unless you consider daily working conditions in the mix. (There has been some difficulty in the past about getting corporate matching grants for employee contributions to gay and lesbian charitable causes, but nearly all employers have cleaned up their acts by accepting any cause with tax-exempt status—a status our groups only won in 1973. Now the employee just has to be brave enough to report the gift.)

The motivation behind the push for domestic-partner benefits is the desire for something symbolic as well as economic. We're looking for validation of our relationships in every way we can. We often don't get it from our biological families. Most religions still won't bless our relationships. And, in this country, most courts and legislatures don't seem likely to allow us the privilege of legal marriage—although a 1993 decision by the highest court in Hawaii has opened the first possibility. We do have domestic-partner registries in a handful of cities (such as Seattle, New York, San Francisco, and Ann Arbor), but the legal benefits and protections are still slim.

That leaves one place where we have some degree of leverage: the workplace. Numerous cases of individuals have demonstrated that when a company really wants you, they'll negotiate. I'm thinking of a lesbian friend, a distinguished scholar who was being anxiously courted for a post at a major university a few years ago. Among what they offered her was a generous mortgage assistance program to purchase a new home when she relocated. She accepted. But when the papers arrived and showed that she intended to own the home jointly with her partner, the university balked—even though the arrangement is routine for spouses. The new professor threatened to cancel the entire arrangement. They signed, but very quietly. They would allow the exception but not change policy. And what we need is policy, so that all of us have equal access.

The economic side, for gay men and lesbians, could be described in simple and familiar terms: equal pay for equal work. But what does it mean for employers? In recent years, discussions about domestic partner benefits have focused almost exclusively on access to health coverage. This, at a time when the U.S. health insurance system is in chaos, all health costs are skyrocketing, and many employees are frantic with anxiety. Not surprisingly, the knee-jerk reaction of many employers is "We can't afford it." That shuts down any attempt for a discussion of an issue that has more angles than just health care. And it overlooks the core issue, which is, just how should an employer support, and define, a family?

The same concerns about employee morale, productivity, and loyalty that spawned diversity efforts have caused employers to look more seriously at "work and family" issues. Workforce diversity means diverse families too. Just as the typical employee is no longer, as the phrase goes, "white, male, and 42 long," the typical family is no longer June staying at home while Ward left to go wherever it was he went to pay the bills. Households with two working parents, single parents with small children, working children caring for elderly parents, unmarried couples (including lesbian and gay couples) with or without children—these have become the norm. Intelligent employers have recognized that stress from home does affect performance on the job and have tried to help alleviate employee concerns with programs such as child care and elder care.

But how do you define a family? This is an issue many good companies are grappling with. A good definition would logically be "the immediate household," but the complexity of legal, biological, and emotional ties could easily involve divorced households or nursing homes and other long-term-care facilities. Meanwhile, those looking toward the bottom line have nightmares about boarding-houses and communes and worry about abuses of the system. Just to complicate matters, these issues are coming to the foreground during the hangover from the free-spending 1980s, while companies are caught up in layoffs, retrenchments, and restructurings. As I often hear, "How can we afford to expand benefits when we're cutting back in so many other ways?"

From a gay and lesbian perspective, domestic-partner benefits don't represent an expansion: they are only a fair application of what already exists. We're willing to accept economic realities in the same spirit as everyone else—grumbling, if that means a cutback in coverage or an increase in employee contribution. But the single most important issue for us is that gay men and lesbians in committed relationships be considered on an equal par with our married colleagues.

Cost issues might be dealt with in less of a panic mode if domestic-partner benefits are looked at in their entirety. Many require no capital outlay at all, just minor adjustments to policy. Even companies in financial straits (no pun intended) can implement benefits that initiate a process toward inclusiveness and equality.

Time

The most basic benefits, bereavement leave and leave to care for a sick partner, are simply a matter of being humane and realistic. Any employer who expects to get work out of people the day after a spouse-equivalent is buried is auditioning for a role in a Dickens novel. But it happens. I know one gay man who nursed his partner almost single-handedly for a full year through the terminal stages of AIDS and never missed a day of work, except for the funeral. The next day, at his desk, he finally broke down. When the story (and he) came out, his supervisor and coworkers were horrified that he had held all this in and never once sought their support. Perhaps you have to be gay to understand his thinking: there was no policy or precedent that said he was entitled to time off and, besides, he was afraid of how his colleagues would react if they knew that his partner was another man. (They were overwhelmingly supportive.) Does anyone ever realize how a policy oversight could result in such an extreme case?

In fact, dozens of companies that offer nothing else

in the way of gay-friendly policies do offer bereavement leave for domestic partners, precisely because of experiences with AIDS and stories like the one above. But since these provisions are not part of a consistent pattern of human resources policy, they tend to get lost over time. When I was told that Time, Inc. (the magazine arm of Time-Warner) had such a policy, I called to confirm. The man I spoke with in the human resources department seemed skeptical, but he offered "to check." The next business day, he called back to say it was true. He sounded genuinely surprised.

Individuals who have a good relationship with a compassionate supervisor have long been able to negotiate leave under these extreme circumstances, but it takes courage at a time when your courage is needed in a lot of other places. A clearly written policy would be genuinely humane. Most organizations have personnel manuals that spell out in excruciating detail the rules for bereavement leave: how many days paid, how many not, how many for a spouse, a parent, a child, a spouse's parent, a sibling, a spouse's sibling, another relative who lived in the same house, etc. A sensible company realizes the emotional and practical ramifications of all these situations. What would it cost to include "domestic partner" on a par with "spouse"? Nothing that wouldn't be paid back in terms of appreciation from the bereaved and of morale among all other employees.

Sick-care leave follows along similar lines, although precise terms are difficult to define since illnesses can vary widely. An opportunity presents itself in the form of the federal Family and Medical Leave Act of 1993. The law mandates up to three months of unpaid leave for the care of family members. Not surprisingly (for anyone familiar with Congress) the definition of "family" doesn't include the partners of lesbians and gay men—as if our situations under those circumstances would be any less demanding. However, gay-friendly companies, while translating the law into company policy, have automatically included domestic partners of lesbian and gay employees, even if the law did not.

This has included the parental-leave aspects surrounding the birth or adoption of a child. Increasingly, we are doing both, but often under unusual legal circumstances because of our inability to marry and because of the erratic homophobia of courts that would rather place children with (closeted and supposedly) single people rather than an openly gay or lesbian couple. We love and care for our children no less than anyone else, perhaps even more, considering what we have to go through. When we get the support of our employers at such a significant time, we don't forget it.

Perks

Beyond these most basic of humane benefits, there is a class of benefits that cost almost as little. These are less connected with issues of great emotional impact but are still a matter of fairness.

The simplest of these concerns access to company events, programs, and facilities. In other words, wherever and whenever spouses are invited, include domestic partners. The most obvious of these are social events, such as the company dinner or the family picnic. Inviting partners as well as spouses (the willing but more squeamish companies state "guest," although this isn't exactly the same message) may seem more a matter of routine than policy. Yet it's a benefit all the same. Of course, at issue is never the cost of the meal (companies have been feeding opposite-sex "beards" for years) but the symbolic value of employees appearing with their same-sex partners.

The July 1993 issue of the *Harvard Business Review* included a full feature on precisely that scenario, in which a star employee, about to be honored at a company dinner, tells his boss that he will be bringing his longtime partner—another man. The boss is caught completely off guard. He wants to be supportive, but, thinking of the event and who will be there, he falls back on a classic homophobic excuse: "What will the clients think?" In the article, seven business experts are asked for their opinions. They all agree that it would be ridiculous to alienate a valued employee by persuading him not to bring his partner. As for the clients, several note that if clients are disturbed by this, enough to endanger their business, then the client relationship was not very stable or healthy to begin with; it could break off on any flimsy excuse. Most clients simply won't care.

Encouraging same-sex domestic partners to attend company events is the ultimate confirmation of a non-discrimination policy; everybody gets the message pretty quickly. And once fairness and honesty are demonstrated in such a high-profile way, it's an easy step to see the importance of applying it consistently in other types of access. Companies vary widely in what they offer in terms of programs and facilities, but what is open to spouses may include fitness facilities, courses and lectures, libraries, travel to conferences (and spousal programs while there), or psychological counseling. (Interestingly, many EAPs—Employee Assistance Programs—for counseling have long included domestic partners, on the theory that if there is trouble at home both halves of a couple needs to be brought into the solution. The decision is made confidentially and on the recommendation of a mental health professional, which is rarely questioned.)

Discounts figure prominently here. Many companies offer spousal or family discounts for their products or services, but few as of yet include domestic partners. Sometimes, it's the result of lawsuits. Woodward and Lothrop, the Washington, D.C., department store (which also owned Garfinckle's) lost a lawsuit brought by a gay employee in the 1980s and was forced to offer domestic-partner discounts equal to those provided spouses. (This never made it a gay-friendly company.) Similar battles are being fought within the major airlines, for discount flying privileges, but few have yet been instituted. Perhaps the most sensible attitude comes from Levi Strauss, which operates a discounted "company store" open to employees and whatever guests the employee invites. As a spokesperson once pointed out to me, their business is selling and promoting their clothing. As long as they're not subsidizing somebody else's retail operation, why not let the employees make the determination?

To round out the fair-and-not-too-expensive category,

I'll toss in issues of relocation. Granted, those eligible are a select and relatively small group, either transferring within the company or taking a job with a new employer that requires a move. The advantage to gay men and lesbians in this situation is that they have unusual leverage: the company really wants them. (I've heard of one company eager enough to promote a gay man to headquarters that they also reassigned his partner, who worked for the company too.) If the recruitment budget included relocation in the first place, there was money to permit a spouse to check out the new turf, shop for a place to live, find schools for the kids, and so on, as well as the actual move. Just because we have to check the "unmarried" box doesn't mean we wouldn't talk over a transfer with our partners. Assuming that the partner agrees with the move and to come along, we shouldn't have to bear that expense ourselves. We deserve equal treatment—and that goes for mortgage assistance or any other program the company may offer. I'm sure this has many other possibilities; once you start examining all policies for heterosexism—and marriage bias—you'll find them.

Insurance

So, finally, we come to the big-ticket items, especially health care. But just how big a ticket are they? Not anywhere near as big as some employers assume. With time, fact is winning out over fear.

The first employer to institute domestic-partner health coverage was *The Village Voice*, a New York–based weekly newspaper, in 1982. Actually, credit for the idea belongs to its union (UAW Local 65) and steward Jeff Weinstein. It was a bad financial year, and the wage offer was low. In an effort to win something, Weinstein put the domestic-partner idea on the table—it included all unmarried couples, gay and not—and management figured, why not? The cost was minimal and it would make the troops happy. The agreement was well received. The plan (for a small company of only 225 employees) is self-insured through the union (and applies only to unionized workers).

The chief concern at that time was the stereotypical perception of "gay promiscuity"—that new partners would be signed up every Monday morning. To prevent this, a one-year waiting period was devised after application before there could be access to coverage. Today, of course, that seems outrageous, but it took the *Voice's* experience to show why: with about twenty couples covered for over a decade, only two have requested a switch of partners, and both were heterosexual.

The successful, pioneering experiment of the *Voice* had few followers (mostly progressive nonprofits) until about 1990, when public employers such as the cities of San Francisco and Seattle adopted coverage for domestic partners; the announcement of Lotus Development in 1991 that it would do so opened the doors at several dozen other private companies. But by that time, two important factors had reared their ugly heads: first, a catastrophic rise in the costs of health care and insurance; second, the devastating impact of the AIDS epidemic on gay men. Both would pose obstacles for domestic-partner health benefits, but especially when the two become confused with one another.

The focus by lesbians and gay men on attaining domestic-partner health benefits has intensified because it is increasingly difficult to gain access to the health-care system—but this problem is one shared by most Americans. The efforts of the Clinton administration to make the system more manageable and accessible hold a lot of promise, but change will take years, and it seems likely that health-care coverage will still be administered primarily through employers (whether this makes sense or not). So, as a gay and lesbian employment issue, partner health coverage is not going to go away.

The most important fact that needs to be recognized—yet is frequently obscured—is that *health coverage for domestic partners costs no more than coverage for spouses.* The proof of this is found in any of the already existing programs, self-insured or not, and most dramatically in the experience of the city of Seattle. When the city informed its insurance carrier that coverage must be provided for domestic partners, the carrier insisted on a surcharge for each partner's premium. After two years, however, the carrier was asked to prove that the additional cost was justified. It couldn't, and the surcharge was rescinded.

These fears, especially from insurance carriers, stem from what can only be described as AIDSphobia. The ignorance and denial surrounding this epidemic, coupled with homophobia, have supported the notion that "if you're gay, you get AIDS." This flies in the face of several facts: that half of the gay community—lesbians—

have one of the lowest incidences of AIDS of any group; that the majority of gay men are not HIV-infected; that gay men in monogamous relationships (remember, we're talking about domestic partners) are at far less risk of infection; that millions of non-gay people around the world have contracted the disease; and that in the United States non-gay people have become the fastest-growing group at risk of infection with the virus. In 1993 heterosexuals took over as the majority of annual new cases. (The enormous role gay men have played in putting the brakes on our own numbers by educating one another is rarely given credit.)

But the prejudices persist, even when insurance companies are asked to look at their own actuarial numbers. Asked what their top concerns are in health-care issues, insurers will answer with the neonatal care of premature babies and problem pregnancies (which can run from $250,000 to $1,000,000 per birth). But this fact does not permit them to discriminate against women of childbearing age. They'll express concern about accidents among teenage dependents (which could result in catastrophic bills for rehabilitation or lifelong therapy and care). But this worry does not permit them to discriminate against parents with children approaching their teen years.

AIDS never appears on those lists of concerns, because the numbers don't support it. The sad fact is that there are few approved drugs or medical therapies available to treat the disease or to run up costs (the cost of the drugs available is also coming down). A commonly accepted figure (from Blue Cross of New York) for the average *lifetime* care of an AIDS patient is $85,000. (Even critics rarely cite a figure higher than $100,000.) This generally reflects hospitalization to treat major infections or complications (which is sporadic, in keeping with the roller-coaster nature of the disease) or represents its terminal phases. In other words, the costs don't go on for long.

As some experts point out, AIDS is a new *type* of disease. It is different from the infectious diseases of the past, such as smallpox or tuberculosis. It's different from cancer, where treatment is often quick or not at all. It's different from the chronic diseases of the heart, lungs, kidneys, and so on, which are the real big-ticket items today. (Funny, nobody ever calls these "lifestyle" diseases, although in many cases they are.)

AIDS is in many ways a combination of all three. For as little as we know about the disease, we do know that the most effective care of HIV infection we have to date is frequent visits to the doctor's office for monitoring and drugs against opportunistic infections. Relative to other diseases, this is not expensive. Those rare, but well-publicized, "million dollar" cases of AIDS are the result of doctors taking the bulldozer approach common to chronic diseases, where every available form of (expensive) technology is employed for lack of options. None of these has ever proven useful.

Some companies have begun to wise up, even when doctors and insurance companies won't. Viacom, for example, has taken the enlightened approach of investigating AIDS costs, criticizing the inflated price of home infusions of medications and repeated hospital admissions when community-based care programs—HIV man-

agement—have proven less expensive and more beneficial to the infected employee (or partner, or spouse).
Viacom's new HIV care program follows these more sensible and cost-effective lines.

Ultimately, the issue with AIDS is not cost per case,
but the incidence of the disease. And we know that incidence can be dramatically reduced with proper education.

Yet insurers—and many health maintenance organizations—persist in opposing domestic-partner health
benefits with some factless argument about AIDS. It's
consistent with stories about insurance companies actually redlining against gay men or even unmarried men
living in certain zip codes. Perhaps it is a reflection, or a
result, of the dismal record the insurance industry as a
whole has in its treatment of its own lesbian and gay employees.

It's too easy to lose domestic-partner benefits in emotional arguments about AIDS. But gay-hostile institutions
have created other obstacles as well. One, surprisingly,
has come from ERISA—federal legislation from the 1970s
that was intended to establish definitions for employee
benefits such as health benefits for spouses and children.
Some companies have refused to provide employees with
domestic-partner health benefits on the grounds that
since this legislation doesn't *require* inclusion of domestic
partners (although it doesn't seem to require much of
anything—that wasn't its purpose) companies don't have
to offer them. Using similar logic, the New York State
Insurance Commission actually *prohibited* carriers in that
state from offering coverage for domestic partners. That

ruling was reversed in September 1993. Other similar kinks exist in the system, but gay-friendly companies, occasionally using their leverage, manage to find solutions. (By the way, the continuation of benefits under COBRA rules—federal legislation from 1985—is the same.)

In figuring costs, the employer should look at what contribution it makes to health benefits for spouses. Remember, the goal here is equality. Some companies pay one hundred percent of spousal benefits, others zero (providing only access to the plan), with plenty of variations in between. This is exactly where the financial burden falls on the gay or lesbian (or other unmarried) *employee*. Under current IRS rules, spousal benefits are tax-exempt; those for domestic partners are not. Fair or not, what that means is that any contribution the employer makes toward coverage is considered taxable income to the employee, and any contribution the employee makes is not tax-deductible. These implications can sometimes skew the economics for the employee and deserve careful consideration.

Just how many employees take advantage of domestic-partner health benefits when they are offered? The numbers are actually small and are partly determined by how the program is defined: some companies offer benefits to all unmarried partners, gay or not; others offer them to lesbian and gay employees only, on the grounds that non-gay employees have the option to marry. (This latter alternative, a recent development, came as a surprise to many gay and lesbian activists who were essentially working against marriage bias, regardless of sexual orientation.)

All-inclusive programs get more applicants, not surprisingly, since the potential pool is larger. Even so, in larger companies the number seems to fix around two percent to three percent of total employees. Levi Strauss estimates that about sixty percent of those who receive the benefit are heterosexual (forty-nine percent are women bringing in male partners, many of whom are self-employed or work for small companies unable to carry decent health coverage). Among city of Seattle employees, the non-gay percentage is about seventy percent. Companies where the benefit is gay-only, such as Lotus, report that only about one percent of employees have taken advantage of the program.

Why so few? The number shouldn't be misinterpreted as indicating that there are few gay or lesbian employees (ten percent is still a reasonable estimate). There are reasonable considerations why more don't apply: 1) Not all of us are in partnerships. (Although various estimates say that sixty to seventy-five percent of us consider ourselves in a "committed relationship," this doesn't always match the definition of "domestic partnership." We'll get to that.) 2) We're more likely to both have jobs, often where coverage for each is equal. 3) The tax situation is a disincentive. 4) Employees are still afraid to come out by signing up. This says much about how gay-friendly policies are working.

So, how do you define a domestic partnership, or—more to the point—how do you prevent abuse of a well-meaning program? The answer is simple: you trust an affidavit, same as with married people. (Do you routinely insist on seeing a marriage license?)

For several years, employers who introduced domestic-partner benefits improvised, often unaware of already existing models. Yet a remarkable similarity evolved, so it was easy to figure out a standard approach. An affidavit for domestic partnership asks the employee to attest to a series of questions or statements that cover three areas.

ESTABLISHING THE RELATIONSHIP:
- The couple resides together and intends to do so indefinitely.
- Both are mutually responsible for basic living expenses.

BASIC LEGAL EXPECTATIONS:
- The couple is not related by blood in a way that would prohibit marriage.
- Both are of the age of consent in the state of residence.
- Neither is married to anyone else.

AGREED TERMS:
- A "statement of termination" will be filed within thirty days (or a reasonable amount of time) upon separation or partner's death.
- A new affidavit for domestic partnership cannot be filed for at least six months after a termination.

These are very reasonable terms, not unlike those expected of a marriage. A company may choose to custom tailor language or terms (legal departments love to fuss with stuff like this) to suit specific situations. It may add a requirement that, if a domestic-partner registry exists in the locality of residence, the couple must register. (Legal registries have been created in a few more than a dozen cities, including San Francisco, New York, Seattle, Minneapolis, Washington, Ann Arbor, West Hollywood, Berkeley, and Madison.) Too many more terms could create unnecessary complications.

Hollywood Supports, the Los Angeles–based educational group, has developed an excellent model form along these lines, that also avoids the potential problem of a stigma attached to a domestic-partnership affidavit. (These forms, like all personnel information, are assumed to be confidential.) Called an Affidavit of Marriage/Spousal Equivalency, it is given to all employees who apply for benefits and covers all circumstances of marriage, common-law marriage, or domestic partnership (gay or not). Unattached employees just don't fill it out—hopefully without any stigma.

The use of forms like this not only clarifies domestic partnerships but should make it simpler for companies to streamline all the benefit policies discussed in this section. A single statement, declaring that all references to "spouse" actually mean "spouse and spouse equivalent (as filed)," could put all the changes in motion. Does this sound too sweeping? Well, we learned how to correct "wife" with "spouse," didn't we?

At the moment, offering domestic-partner health benefits to lesbian and gay employees seems like the zenith of gay-friendliness. However, there is still another area of contention brewing: pension and survivor benefits and similar contributory investments. Some of the benefits a company offers employees, such as life insurance, can be assigned to any beneficiary. (Or so I thought. More and more instances arise of life insurance companies insisting on "blood relatives" as beneficiaries. They need to be more publicly embarrassed about this.) Others, such as stock options, can be converted into joint ownership or transferred under the terms of a will. (Gay men and lesbians have no automatic legal standing as survivors in a partner's estate; terms have to be spelled out and specific. Even then, blood relatives have been known to contest and win.) But some financial benefits are dispensed in a discriminatory fashion as a matter of company policy.

This was illustrated in the legal battle of *Rovira vs. AT&T.* Following the death of Marjorie Forlini, a vested AT&T employee, her life partner, Sandra Rovira, filed for survivor benefits, a lump-sum payment the company routinely distributes to a spouse after an employee's death, that represents the contributed amount toward a pension that won't be collected. Forlini and Rovira had been a couple for over twelve years, owned a home together, and raised Rovira's children together—but AT&T refused the request. By their rules, the survivor's benefit went to a legal spouse or no one. Rovira sued, on the grounds that AT&T was violating its own well-known policy of not discriminating on the basis of sexual orientation. After four years of litigation, the case was resolved in 1993. Rovira lost.

Naturally, the unfairness of not being able to control

what happens to your pension investment when you can't have it yourself annoyed many gay men and lesbians. However, the implications of the Rovira case seem to have been obscured by the more popular push for health benefits (as have the problems with the Pentagon, in Colorado, in Oregon, and numerous other fronts). My prediction is that, with the aging of Baby Boomer activists, you haven't seen the last of this issue.

As is frequently the case with lesbian and gay employment issues, our concerns parallel much larger, more general problems. In the case of domestic-partner benefits, what's revealed is the growing crisis concerning how employers will deal with benefits of any kind amid the changes in the economy, the society, the family, and the individual. Just what are the responsibilities of business? What's really needed? Child care? Elder care? Health care? Education? What's going to attract and retain the best employees? What does business need in order to thrive? What's all this going to cost? And how are we going to pay for it?

Business is going to have to reexamine its entire approach toward benefits. Some experts, such as Per Larson, the New York–based financial planner who once headed marketing in the benefits consulting group at the CPA firm Coopers & Lybrand, suggest that a logical solution might be found in a "cafeteria plan," in which each employee is given a dollar amount and allowed to shop through a menu of possible benefits, selecting what each needs or prefers. What once would have been a logistical nightmare has become, with improved technology and software, a significant pathway through the old, homogenized, one-size-fits-all philosophy of business. The result: a vibrant, responsive new system that gets the best for and from each individual.

When business is ready to face up to that, we gay men and lesbians will be at the table—not only with our expectations, but with creative and practical ideas for making it all work. As we always are.

Safety, Acceptance, Equality

When I heard about a video being circulated by right-wing extremists in Oregon, Colorado, and even in Queens, New York, something called "The Homosexual Agenda," my first reaction was, "Gee, somebody came up with an agenda? How come I haven't heard about it?"

Of course, the video was another typical piece of propaganda, brimming with hate and planned to inspire fear. We would have to answer it with another video, filled with patience and love, facts and testimonials. (Fortunately, Dee Mosbacher, Frances Reid, and the good people at Parents and Friends of Lesbians and Gays are doing just that.) And the back-and-forth will continue.

But it got me thinking: just what *is* the gay and lesbian agenda? We see so many manifestos and lists of objectives at marches and in handbills—so much to remember, so much to think about.

Then it occurred to me. What so many lesbians and gay men have told me about what they need in the workplace, what they're worried about—the conversations that helped me draw up the objectives set out in this chapter—this is what it comes down to: safety, acceptance, equality.

Looking at ourselves from a national perspective, we are all at different points in our lives, working in different circumstances, caught between fear and courage—it's confusing. But, in fact, we're all just at different levels on a three-step stair. Safety, acceptance, equality. We need all of them. But we're going to get them only one step at a time.

We shouldn't be surprised to find that employers also are at different places on the stair. We haven't been at this very long. We've had to learn that we change the law with the power of our votes. That we change the courts with the power of our persistence and faith in our own rights. That we change public opinion with the power of our own testimonials. In the same way, we will change the workplace with the power of our talent, experience, creativity, and the respect we've earned by doing a job well—as long as we take the brave leap to link those valued assets with the open fact that we are . . . different. Let me say it: Queer.

Any company that shows a willingness to work with us on these issues, to help us do our jobs better, deserves credit, no matter where it is on this three-step stair. But it's the companies who see that it is in their own best interests to do so—to take our concerns into the very heart of their culture, and break out, as each of us must do, of that destructive, shaming silence—well, these are the companies that deserve to be called gay-friendly. And these are the companies we will help make stars.

Backlash

Just when you thought it was getting safe to be honest . . .

In late 1993, as this book was being completed, three of the five commissioners of Williamson County, Texas, voted to deny Apple Computer a standard $750,000 tax abatement for its proposed $80 million facility. Their reasons were explicit: they did not approve of Apple's gay-friendly policies, specifically the equal benefits for unmarried couples. They did not want gay people, or their friends, or apparently their employers, in their community.

At the time, I immediately detected a new frostiness from some of the companies I was speaking with for this book. Some were very reluctant to talk or to confirm information. As one put it bluntly, "What are you creating? A hit list for the fundamentalists?"

No business likes controversy. I appreciate that. But at the same time, it's not beneficial to bury your head in the sand. Eventually, choices have to be made.

Apple was forced to make a choice. To its credit, it made a business choice based on facts. It looked at its workforce, whom it comprised, what they gave the company, what they needed back. And it looked at Williamson County, with a $750,000 carrot and its local attitudes laid bare. Which was the right investment?

Apple picked up its planned $80 million investment, the one thousand new jobs, and announced it would build someplace else. It had no shortage of options.

One week later, the Williamson County commissioners (said to be under pressure from sources ranging from local constituents to Texas governor Ann Richards) reversed themselves. Well, there was room for saving face. They offered Apple a different incentive package, totaling nearly a million dollars. Apple accepted.

Would this mark the end of any nagging fears companies have about backlash against gay and lesbian progress? I asked the opinion of a Texas-based manager for another high-tech company, who also happens to be a lesbian. Her assessment was upbeat. As she summarized, "Folks here in Texas think mighty poorly of what those commissioners tried to do. And nobody likes to be thought of poorly in Texas."

II

Companies

What are some companies that welcome
gay and lesbian workers?
That value talent over prejudice?
That are ready for a new business future?
Who are the role models?

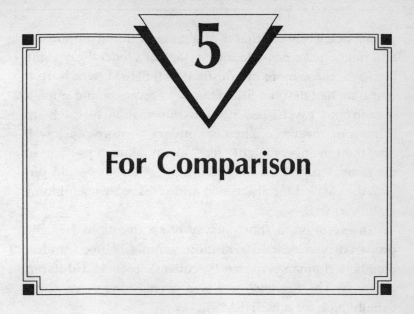

5

For Comparison

There is precious little hard data on the actual situation of lesbian and gay employees in American companies. Although various individuals and a few organizations have been collecting information over time, to date only two actual surveys of any size or reliability have been conducted, one by the Society for Human Resource Management (SHRM) and the other by the Workplace Project of the National Gay and Lesbian Task Force (NGLTF), both in 1993. (A third, conducted by the New York–based Wall Street Project, was in progress while this book was being written. Results are expected in 1994.)

The SHRM survey (January–February 1993) grew out of a meeting I had with representatives from the fifty-thousand-member professional association in late 1992. Their

primary concern was that the incoming Clinton administration might make possible the passage of a federal gay-rights
law. (Ah, those more optimistic days!) SHRM, which up to
that time had devoted little energy to diversity and none to
lesbian and gay issues, needed information to catch up.
(Thus our meeting.) Their secondary concern was, well,
how their members might "feel" about taking a position on
the issue. I suggested they ask them. A survey would provide the catalyst for discussion and yield some useful information as well.

In execution, a short survey of six questions (which I
prepared) was sent to a random sample of five hundred
members (human resource executives), each in a different
company. The response rate was twenty-nine percent, un-
usually high for any SHRM survey.

In summary, the survey found that 63 percent of companies had "widely understood" policies against discrimination on the basis of sexual orientation. However, only 38
percent had *written* policies that stated the same. One-third
of the respondents (34 percent) said their companies had
workforce diversity programs, but less than half (16 percent)
included gay and lesbian issues within their context. Less
than 5 percent reported having a gay and lesbian employee group.

In terms of benefits, the SHRM survey found that about
10 percent offered bereavement leave for the death of a domestic partner, and almost the same percentage offered
spousal discounts or access to company programs and facilities to the partners while they were alive. About 5 percent
offered relocation assistance, and only 2 percent offered
health coverage. (Of the respondents with any of these

benefits, all reported "no change" in their costs except one, who reported a slight increase.)

SHRM issued the survey with a positive spin, and its board subsequently issued a resolution supporting non-discrimination and pointedly not taking a stand on domestic-partner benefits. By then, congressional debate on gay men and lesbians in the military had exploded, making any type of gay-rights bill unlikely, so SHRM seemed to lose all interest in the issue.

The NGLTF survey, conducted by a California-based group of volunteers, was begun in July 1993 and concentrated on Fortune 1000 companies only. By October, when preliminary results were released, about 25 percent of the one thousand had responded. However, only 10 percent agreed to participate. The remaining 15 percent responded by refusing to participate.

The results from that sample were dramatically different. Nearly 72 percent of participants reported having a written non-discrimination policy, and well over half (58 percent) included gay and lesbian issues in diversity training. About 21 percent had recognized gay and lesbian employee groups (no accounting could be made of unrecognized groups), and 5 percent offered domestic-partner benefits that included health-care coverage.

The problem with these initial figures, of course, is that the survey isn't yet complete. Companies dealing actively with lesbian and gay issues were more likely to respond quickly and affirmatively. (Even so, a quick review of the respondent list showed some notably gay-friendly companies missing.) Also, we're not sure about company reactions to a gay-sponsored study (those resistant could have larger problems). Nor is it clear how representative the Fortune 1000 is of all American employees on lesbian and gay concerns. The NGLTF study will continue into 1994, at which time more comprehensive information should be available.

The actual picture may not be as rosy as that shown by the initial NGLTF figures nor as dismal as that depicted by SHRM. The situation is also changing rapidly. Only one thing is absolutely certain: we need more facts. Keep them coming.

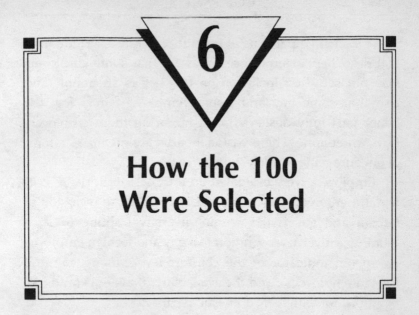

How the 100 Were Selected

The list provided here doesn't pretend to be a scientific study. The companies were located journalistically over a period of three years (1991–93) through networks and referrals, published reports, word of mouth, and sometimes just a hunch. Most companies, but not all, agreed to cooperate. Efforts were made to speak both with management and with lesbian and gay employees to obtain a balanced picture, but this was not always possible. Details are provided only where reliable information from within the company was available. Information only from outside sources is summarized or noted as anecdotal.

My goal in assembling this list was twofold: to show gay men and lesbians some of the employment options we have and to give credit to employers who are making an honest effort to change patterns of institutionalized discrimination that elsewhere are routine. I'm aware that some employers may not see their inclusion on this list as an honor (and also that some gay and lesbian employees may feel the honor isn't fully deserved), but honoring these employers is the intention. (The occasional barbs are meant as a form of encouragement, okay?)

Employers were evaluated on four basic criteria: a written and enforced policy of non-discrimination; inclusion of lesbian and gay issues within diversity training (if such training is given); recognition of a gay and lesbian employee group (an indicator of the comfort level among gay and lesbian employees); and the availability of benefits (and recognition) for same-sex domestic partners.

Obviously, at this point in history, if I looked for perfect scores in all categories, I'd have an extremely limited sample. But a long-term process of change is involved here, and I think all the employers listed are somewhere in that process. To help differentiate among them, I've included ratings of *excellent*, *good*, and *trying* to indicate to what point they've advanced. The triangles (color them pink), on a scale of one to five, are intended to convey a sense of overall gay-friendliness.

Since I've also tried to present as much diversity as possible in terms of industry, geography, type of company, size, and other factors, there's something of a weighting system involved. High-tech industries and higher education are moving faster than most, so I have a tendency to be tougher on them, while areas such as chemicals and accounting are a bit behind, so I'm more generous. I have no delusions of objectivity. My greatest regret is that in many fields I was unable to find any representatives at all. Where are you?

In terms of geography, there's a definite skew toward big cities and especially toward the West Coast and the Northeast Corridor. This is where the greatest amount of activity is occurring. However, there are also splendid companies located throughout the heartland, and I've made a special effort to find them. My biggest problem has been the South. It's not that there aren't gay-friendly companies based there, but that they are terrified of being portrayed as such. Some are even doing courageous advocacy work behind the scenes in hostile political and social environments—they feared I could do more damage than good by including them. While I may be "outing" other companies that have nothing to lose but their own fears, I had to accept these concerns as valid—for now. Our southern friends and colleagues still have options with employers located in the South but based elsewhere.

This list is far from definitive, but it's a start. I'm certain I have missed some excellent companies that deserve recognition and others just starting the process of inclusion. We need to hear from you. Nothing would please me more than to see a larger, improved edition of this book in the future.

There are probably some out there who may read this book to cause mischief. If this is your intent, I ask that you read the book through, consider its message, and realize that the process of change I talk about is no longer reversible. Otherwise, I hope that you paid full price.

And for those of you who understand the message and who have contact with any of the companies listed: do us all a favor. Congratulate them.

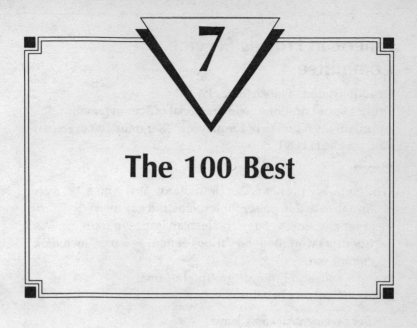

The 100 Best

American Friends Service Committee ▽▽▽▽▽

Headquartered: **Philadelphia, PA**
Other Major Locations: **Nine regional offices nationally**
Approximate Number of Employees: **200 (plus 200 overseas)**
Rating: **EXCELLENT**

Written policy prohibits discrimination: **Yes, with a 1978 af-firmative-action policy for lesbians and gay men**
Includes awareness of gay and lesbian issues in training: **Yes (sponsors workshops on various employee issues, including coming out)**
Lesbian and gay employee group: **Informal**
Domestic-partner benefits:

> **Bereavement/sickness leave**
> **Relocation assistance**
> **Health coverage**

This organization, which runs the earthly affairs of the religious Society of Friends (better known as Quakers), is small but has full equality in everything it offers. (It just doesn't *have* a dental plan. And discounts don't apply here.) It's been a real advocate for domestic-partner medical benefits, getting out the facts. As for "lavender ceiling" issues: no less than eight members of its board of directors are openly gay or lesbian.

American Psychological Association

∨∨∨∨∨

Headquartered: **Washington, DC**
Approximate Number of Employees: **400**
Rating: **EXCELLENT**

Written policy prohibits discrimination: **Yes**
Includes awareness of gay and lesbian issues in training: **Yes**
Lesbian and gay employee group: **Yes**
Domestic-partner benefits:

Bereavement/sickness leave
Employee Assistance Program/counseling
Health coverage

It took some hard lobbying and persuasion in the 1970s to convince the APA to take a more objective look at homosexuality and remove it from the official list of "disorders." But once the message got through, the rest came naturally. The APA adopted domestic-partner health benefits (for its staff and for its 14,000 members) as early as 1983. The number of openly gay and lesbian staff is large and comfortable.

American Telephone & Telegraph Co. (AT&T)

∇∇∇∇

Headquartered: **Basking Ridge, NJ**
Other Major Locations: **Everywhere**
Approximate Number of Employees: **300,000**
Rating: **GOOD**

Written policy prohibits discrimination: **Yes, since 1975**
Includes awareness of gay and lesbian issues in training: **Yes, extensively**
Lesbian and gay employee group: **LEAGUE (Lesbian & Gay United Employees)**
Domestic-partner benefits: **None**

No company has had such a strong reputation as gay-friendly for as long as Ma Bell, hiring without discrimination long before this became formal policy and fostering the most extensive lesbian and gay infrastructure in the business world. AT&T also pioneered homophobia awareness training in the workplace, starting in the mid 1980s. It regularly invites speakers for "Gay Awareness Week." The problem, I hate to bring this up, is that it all looks great on paper but doesn't translate into practice—probably because there's no real support at the top of the corporate echelons. Attitudes vary by division (research is the best—the old Bell Labs). Your own position depends almost entirely on who your supervisor is, so many closets are locked tight. And the company's legal stand against domestic-partner benefits was a real letdown to many. Insiders say we'll have to wait a few more years until the old guard retires; progressive management is in the wings. If the company could recognize the loyal boosters (and salespeople!) it has in LEAGUE, it would happen even faster.

Andersen Consulting/
Arthur Andersen & Co. ▽▽

Headquartered: **Chicago, IL**
Other Major Locations: **Worldwide**
Approximate Number of Employees: **12,500 (25,000 world-
wide)**
Rating: **TRYING**

Written policy prohibits discrimination: **Yes, since 1992**
Includes awareness of gay and lesbian issues in training: **Yes**
Lesbian and gay employee group: **ANGLES**
Domestic-partner benefits: **None**

The more progressive (and arguably more in-touch) consulting division of this giant international accounting
firm just might lead its audit-and-tax parent toward
greater enlightenment—and set a much needed example
for the rest of the Big Six. Andersen Consulting provided
the model for a diversity task force (inclusive of lesbian
and gay issues), and will soon be launching educational
programs. The still-young employee group (which is not
formally recognized by the firm) is optimistic, and cites
the (moral) support it receives from upper management.

Apple Computer Inc.   ▽▽▽▽▽

Headquartered: **Cupertino, CA**
Other Major Locations: **Colorado, Texas, and Virginia**
Approximate Number of Employees: **14,500**
Rating: **EXCELLENT**

Written policy prohibits discrimination: **Yes, since 1988**
Includes awareness of gay and lesbian issues in training: **Yes
    (programs included in management training at Apple U.,
    also available on demand)**
Lesbian and gay employee group: **Apple Lambda**
Domestic-partner benefits:

   **Access to company events and facilities
   Bereavement/sickness leave
   Employee Assistance Program/counseling
   Discounts
   Relocation assistance
   Health coverage
   Dental plan
   Adoption benefits**

Although some veterans recall that it wasn't all that easy, Apple has rapidly moved forward to become one of the standard-bearers among gay-friendly companies. It's not just the fully-equal benefits policy—Lambda members deserve special credit for winning them one by one, in a sensible and persistent strategy—but also the increasing comfort level of high-ranking, lesbian and gay executives. This encourages them not only to come out, but to take visible leadership positions in our community. Consistency counts, too. Apple hasn't backed down from, hidden, or apologized for any of its gay-friendly policies in the face of anti-gay backlash.

Arizona Public Service   ▽▽▽▽▽

Headquartered: **Phoenix, AZ**
Other Major Locations: **Throughout Arizona**
Approximate Number of Employees: **7,000**
Rating: **GOOD**

Written policy prohibits discrimination: **Yes, since 1991**
Includes awareness of gay and lesbian issues in training: **Yes**
Lesbian and gay employee group: **None**
Domestic-partner benefits:

> **Access to company events and facilities**
> **Bereavement/sickness leave**

Arizona may not have a reputation as a gay-friendly environment, but the company that delivers electricity to 70 percent of the state is getting one. Much of the credit belongs to a remarkable CEO, who is powering an effort to flatten the organization, create more effective, cross-departmental teams, and otherwise develop a "leading edge" utility. Diversity figures prominently here: Monthly "breakthrough leadership workshops," with a strong message of inclusiveness, have "spread through the company like wildfire." So it seems the message is getting through. The company has even taken a stand in political battles of an anti-gay nature (militant fundamentalists are mounting an Oregon- and Colorado-style assault); some say even to the "lending" of lobbyists to help the lesbian and gay defense. When Barry Goldwater announced his support of the Phoenix gay-rights law in 1992, the press conference was hosted by the CEO of Arizona Public Service. It isn't known how many fundamentalists refused to turn on their lights that night.

The ASK Group   ▽▽▽▽▽

Headquartered: **Santa Clara, CA**
Other Major Locations: **Santa Rosa, Alameda, and worldwide**
Approximate Number of Employees: **1,500 (2,400 worldwide)**
Rating: **EXCELLENT**

Written policy prohibits discrimination: **Yes, since 1991**
Includes awareness of gay and lesbian issues in training: **In development**
Lesbian and gay employee group: **Informal (company recognizes no groups)**
Domestic-partner benefits:

> **Access to company events and facilities**
> **Bereavement/sickness leave**
> **Employee Assistance Program/counseling**
> **Relocation assistance**
> **Health coverage (includes partner's children)**
> **Dental plan**
> **Vision plan**

Keeping up with the rest of Silicon Valley, this maker of business application software offers a pretty good package of benefits but is quick to point out that it "doesn't advocate any kind of relationship"—everything is equal for everyone, gay or not, married or not. Unfortunately, the rest of the business world doesn't feel the same: ASK has to pay a surcharge to HMOs if partners opt for that version of health coverage. (Could someone please explain why?) The name of the company, by the way, has nothing to do with questioning. It's the initials of its founders' names.

Bank of America   ▽

Headquartered: **San Francisco, CA**
Other Major Locations: **Worldwide**
Approximate Number of Employees: **80,000 in the U.S.**
Rating: **TRYING**

Written policy prohibits discrimination: **Yes**
Includes awareness of gay and lesbian issues in training: **Yes**
Lesbian and gay employee group: **None**
Domestic-partner benefits: **(said to be working on upgrade)**

   Bereavement/sickness leave

So, how do you tell the difference between being responsive to gay employees and, say, basic marketing sense? Or just damage control? BankAmeria is still carrying a black eye for withholding funding from the local Boy Scouts (because of their insistence on discriminating against gay scouts and leaders) and then changing its mind. Still, it's been generous to the local lesbian and gay community, and openly gay employees seem to do okay. Compared to Citicorp, Bank of America looks like Wigstock.

Ben & Jerry's Homemade Inc. ▽▽▽▽▽

Headquartered: **Waterbury, VT**
Approximate Number of Employees: **600**
Rating: **EXCELLENT**

Written policy prohibits discrimination: **Yes**
Includes awareness of gay and lesbian issues in train-
ing: **No training**
Lesbian and gay employee group: **None**
Domestic-partner benefits:

Bereavement/sickness leave
Health coverage
Dental plan
Adoption benefits

Whose "best" list *doesn't* include Ben & Jerry's? Well, they
make this one too. Non-discrimination isn't so much policy as a way of life. Diversity training is seen as something
redundant, since the company devotes energy and
profits to nearly every socially responsible human (and
environmental) cause known. Instead of employee
groups, they have their "Joy Gang," a committee dedi-
cated to spreading joy at work. Benefits were equalized
in 1989 (among the earliest). Gay and lesbian issues just
aren't an issue here—which could be something of an
ideal. Plus you get your ice cream and frozen yogurt free.

Blue Cross and Blue Shield of Massachusetts ▽▽▽▽▽

Headquartered: **Boston, MA**
Other Major Locations: **Throughout Massachusetts and Maine**
Approximate Number of Employees: **6,000**
Rating: **EXCELLENT**

Written policy prohibits discrimination: **Yes**
Includes awareness of gay and lesbian issues in training: **Yes, for all employees**
Lesbian and gay employee group: **Informal only**
Domestic-partner benefits:

> **Access to company events and facilities**
> **Bereavement/sickness leave**
> **Employee Assistance Program/counseling**
> **Health coverage**
> **Dental plan**
> **Pension permits named beneficiary**

"We want to be the employer of choice, as well as the insurer of choice," the company says. With its inclusive diversity roundtable, its annual celebration of Gay Pride Month every June (one of its regular "cultural months") and its record of promoting openly gay and lesbian managers to upper ranks, this insurer has a comfortable reputation as a gay-friendly environment. Its strongest statement came with the adoption of full domestic-partner benefits in late 1993—the first major insurance company to offer partner health coverage to both employees and customers (the latter since 1991). "In the past two years, we found that this benefit was not administratively complex or costly. Employers and insurance consultants have found the claims experience for domestic partners has been the same as for married or single employees."

The Body Shop Inc. ▽▽

Headquartered: **Wake Forest, NC**
Other Major Locations: **New Jersey, California, Florida, and Ontario**
Approximate Number of Employees: **600**
Rating: **TRYING**

___

Written policy prohibits discrimination: **Yes**
Includes awareness of gay and lesbian issues in training: **No**
Lesbian and gay employee group: **None**
Domestic-partner benefits: **None**

The Body Shop, the darling of everybody else's socially responsible list, is said to be a supportive environment, and there are openly gay representatives in upper management, but there still seems to be a problem here. While there is some inclusion of gay issues within AIDS-awareness education, it's missing on the diversity side. (There are reports that the company "backed off" from inclusion because Amnesty International generally abstains from lesbian and gay issues, especially in the United States.) While the company says it's "looking into" a health plan that would cover domestic partners, no related policy exists on other benefits. Still, it gets extra credit for being in North Carolina. (The number of employees shown is for corporate headquarters and forty-four company-owned stores. An additional 123 stores are franchises and not included here.)

Borland International Inc.   ▽▽▽▽

Headquartered: **Scotts Valley, CA**
Other Major Locations: **Worldwide**
Approximate Number of Employees: **1,000 (1,900 worldwide)**
Rating: **GOOD**

___

Written policy prohibits discrimination: **Yes**
Includes awareness of gay and lesbian issues in training: **No**
Lesbian and gay employee group: **None (company has no employee groups)**
Domestic-partner benefits:

> **Access to company events and facilities**
> **Bereavement/sickness leave**
> **Relocation assistance**
> **Health coverage**
> **Dental plan**

Like most of its high-tech neighbors in the Silicon Valley area, software maker Borland has a fine selection of domestic-partner benefits. In this industry, it's a matter of business necessity; rival companies are recruiting talent in a highly competitive market. It seems a comfortable enough place to be out, but the company seems a bit nervous about "activists," including your own mild-mannered reporter.

The Boston Globe ▽▽▽▽▽

Headquartered: **Boston, MA**
Approximate Number of Employees: **3,400**
Rating: **EXCELLENT**

The *Globe* refused to give us any details for this book, but it's been pretty well publicized that it offers its gay and lesbian employees partner health coverage and bereavement leave for the death of a domestic partner— maybe more. Employees seem to sense an ambivalence too. None of this seems to be affected by the *Globe's* 1993 operating merger with *The New York Times,* which isn't known to offer either. And the *Times* won't talk.

Bureau of National Affairs Inc.   ▽▽▽▽

Headquartered: **Washington, DC**
Approximate Number of Employees: **1,500**
Rating: **GOOD**

Written policy prohibits discrimination: **Yes, since the late 1980s**
Includes awareness of gay and lesbian issues in training: **Yes, in both diversity and sexual-harassment programs**
Lesbian and gay employee group: **An informal network (originated by women with a newspaper ad calling for "LesBNA")**
Domestic-partner benefits:

**Bereavement/sickness leave
(Health coverage under negotiation)**

A 100 percent employee-owned publishing firm (electronic and print) that specializes in reporting on government regulations, BNA has long been one of the major nongovernmental employers in the Washington area—thus something of a magnet for lesbian and gay talent. It did a lot for the credibility of domestic-partner benefits when it became the first mainstream organization to study, track, and report on employers who adopted them. It's nice to have this kind of ally. Now BNA just has to equalize its own benefits policies. Management seems open to discussion. Some are out themselves.

Celestial Seasonings Inc. ▽

Headquartered: **Boulder, CO**
Approximate Number of Employees: **220**
Rating: **TRYING**

Written policy prohibits discrimination: **Yes**
Includes awareness of gay and lesbian issues in training: **Yes,
for supervisors**
Lesbian and gay employee group: **None**
Domestic-partner benefits: **None (but said to be shopping)**

Even though there are some activists still boycotting its teas (because of a questionable accusation that it's "not done enough" against Colorado's odious Amendment 2), the record at Celestial Seasonings is okay. This is a small, funky company (that's much happier since it rebought itself from Kraft) with some "vocal" gay and lesbian members on the management team. It may not suit everyone's tastes, but those who work here seem to like it. Besides, the way I see it, just *being* progressive in Colorado these days deserves extra credit.

Children's Hospital of Boston ▽▽▽▽▽

Headquartered: **Boston, MA**
Approximate Number of Employees: **4,200**
Rating: **EXCELLENT**

Written policy prohibits discrimination: **Yes**
Includes awareness of gay and lesbian issues in training: **Yes**
Lesbian and gay employee group: **Informal committee**
Domestic-partner benefits:

>**Access to company events and facilities**
>**Bereavement/sickness leave**
>**Employee Assistance Program/counseling**
>**Health coverage**
>**Dental plan**

Come by in June—Gay Pride Month, of course—and see the lobby display on lesbian and gay rights. You'll get a pretty clear picture of just how gay-friendly they are here. The informal lesbian and gay committee meets monthly, takes an active role in diversity programs, but keeps a decidedly low profile—which seems to have more to do with the state of the health-care professions than with the climate at this institution. Benefits were equalized fully in 1991.

Children's Television Workshop ▽▽▽

Headquartered: **New York, NY**
Approximate Number of Employees: **400**
Rating: **GOOD**

Written policy prohibits discrimination: **Yes**
Includes awareness of gay and lesbian issues in training: **No training ("we don't need it")**
Lesbian and gay employee group: **None**
Domestic-partner benefits:

> **Access to company events and facilities**
> **Bereavement/sickness leave**
> **Employee Assistance Program/counseling**

The producers of *Sesame Street* (and other slightly less legendary TV programs) have preached acceptance of differences of all types for decades, and they carry it through into the workplace as well. Where else could you work if you were Big Bird? While there seems to be a certain degree of nervousness about publicly acknowledging its gay-friendly policies (could it be the old inability to equate "gay" with "family"?), CTW delivers. When it can offer full and fair health and dental benefits (said to be in the works), it will deserve the highest rating. Stay tuned.

CMP Publications Inc.   ▽▽▽▽▽

Headquartered: **Manhasset, NY**
Other Major Locations: **California, Texas, and Illinois**
Approximate Number of Employees: **1,100**
Rating: **EXCELLENT**

Written policy prohibits discrimination: **Yes**
Includes awareness of gay and lesbian issues in training: **Yes**
Lesbian and gay employee group: **Informal only**
Domestic-partner benefits:

> **Bereavement/sickness leave**
> **Employee Assistance Program/counseling**
> **Health coverage**
> **Dental plan**

Management has taken a pretty open and direct approach to dealing with gay and lesbian issues at this computer magazine publisher, enacting a range of policies in a short time. (Benefits are for same-sex couples only. Some of the health plan choices also cover the partner's kids.) Not that lesbian and gay employees had any complaints before. Ah, but it's that sense of competition for the best talent. They want it, whatever it takes. Nice to see a bit of Silicon Valley on Long Island.

Colgate Palmolive Co.   ▽▽▽

Headquartered: **New York, NY**
Other Major Locations: **Worldwide**
Approximate Number of Employees: **8,000**
Rating: **GOOD**

Written policy prohibits discrimination: **Yes, since 1993**
Includes awareness of gay and lesbian issues in training: **In process**
Lesbian and gay employee group: **Informal only**
Domestic-partner benefits: **Under review**

Perhaps because it is such a high-profile consumer products company, Colgate is making changes very quietly— but very rapidly. Within only a year, a discrimination policy was elucidated, lesbian and gay issues were added to its existing diversity task force, and recommendations were put forth for equalizing benefits (unresolved at press time)—but no one will talk about what's driving the process. Madge, maybe? Well, whatever it is, it's working.

Columbia University   ∨∨∨∨∨

Headquartered: **New York, NY**
Approximate Number of Employees: **14,000**
Rating: **EXCELLENT**

Written policy prohibits discrimination: **Yes**
Includes awareness of gay and lesbian issues in training: **Yes**
Lesbian and gay employee group: **GaBLES (Gay, Bisexual & Lesbian Employees and Students), among others**
Domestic-partner benefits:

> **Access to company events and facilities**
> **Bereavement/sickness leave**
> **Health coverage**
> **Dental plan**

When Manhattan's Ivy League extended health benefits to same-sex partners of non-union employees (faculty, administrators) in late 1993 (unionized employees had negotiated them earlier) it rounded out an admirable, longtime record as a gay-friendly employer. (It even managed to strong-arm recalcitrant HMOs into cooperating.) In terms of employment, don't forget there's more than the school: there are the hospitals, the press, and the Lamont-Doherty Observatory as well.

Commonwealth Edison Co.   ▽

Headquartered: **Chicago, IL**
Other Major Locations: **Throughout Illinois**
Approximate Number of Employees: **18,700**
Rating: **TRYING**

Written policy prohibits discrimination: **Yes**
Includes awareness of gay and lesbian issues in training: **No training**
Lesbian and gay employee group: **Informal only**
Domestic-partner benefits: **None**

Can time cure even the homophobia of utility companies? With a bit of pressure from outside and inside, they learn to listen. It's happening at Chicago's electric company. It's just begun to explore the idea of diversity programs. But employees have already started having a Commonwealth Edison float in Chicago's Gay Pride Day Parade.

CoreStates Bank N.A.   ▽▽▽

Headquartered: **Philadelphia, PA**
Other Major Locations: **Subsidiary banks in Pennsylvania, New Jersey, New York, and Delaware**
Approximate Number of Employees: **13,000**
Rating: **GOOD**

Written policy prohibits discrimination: **Yes**
Includes awareness of gay and lesbian issues in training: **Recently started**
Lesbian and gay employee group: **"Mosaic"**
Domestic-partner benefits: **None**

Management is said to be struggling with lesbian and gay issues here—they certainly seem uncomfortable talking about us—but a new diversity plan (and its perpetrators) seem determined to be inclusive. The intriguingly named lesbian and gay employee group provides much in the way of education and support.

CUNA Mutual Insurance Group   ▽▽▽

Headquartered: **Madison, WI**
Other Major Locations: **Michigan, Iowa, California, and nationwide**
Approximate Number of Employees: **5,000**
Rating: **GOOD**

Written policy prohibits discrimination: **Yes**
Includes awareness of gay and lesbian issues in training: **Getting there**
Lesbian and gay employee group: **Gay & Lesbian Employees of CUNA Mutual**
Domestic-partner benefits:

> **Access to company events and facilities**
> **Bereavement/sickness leave (union members only; unequal: you get three days off for death of a spouse or parent, two days for domestic partner or grandparent) (Cute)**

The company sends a pretty strong message out about not discriminating—which may not be such a bad idea for one of the largest private employers in the People's Republic of Madison—but let's not pretend it's easy being different here. This *is* an insurance company. (CUNA Mutual provides insurance to credit union members: credit insurance, bonding, property, casualty, individual life, and health policies. No, it doesn't offer policies to member's domestic partners. It hasn't noticed the market yet.) The company is in the process of reexamining its benefits (mostly geared to cutbacks), and a possible switch to a cafeteria-type plan may open opportunities for equal benefits, at least for nonunion personnel.

Dayton Hudson Corp. ▽

Headquartered: **Minneapolis, MN**
Other Major Locations: **Stores in thirty-three states**
Approximate Number of Employees: **160,000**
Rating: **TRYING**

Written policy prohibits discrimination: **Yes**
Includes awareness of gay and lesbian issues in training: **Yes, varies by division**
Lesbian and gay employee group: **None**
Domestic-partner benefits: **None**

What's confusing about Dayton Hudson (and what may make it difficult for lesbian and gay employees to come together) is the decentralization of about eight hundred stores, organized in three separate divisions (there are only about two hundred employees at headquarters). The department store division (Dayton's, Hudson's, and Marshall Field) seems a bit stodgy but may be ripe for change, as employees ask; Mervyn's, mostly in California, has a mixed reputation for gay-friendliness; and Target, the discount division, has been tarred for keeping an AIDS book off its shelves (though this may have little to do with employment practices). While on the whole this looks better than most other major retailers, without strong direction from the top, each store pretty much sets its own spin on policy. Tread carefully.

Digital Equipment Corp. (DEC) ▽▽▽▽

Headquartered: **Maynard, MA**
Oher Major Locations: **Worldwide**
Approximate Number of Employees: **90,000 (113,000 world-wide)**
Rating: **GOOD**

Written policy prohibits discrimination: **Yes, since mid-1980s**
Includes awareness of gay and lesbian issues in training: **Yes (one of the pioneers).**
Lesbian and gay employee groups: **Numerous. DECplus (people like us), DEC PAC (Policy Action Committee), QWAD (Queers Working at Digital); less officially, WICS (Women in Comfortable Shoes); others**
Domestic-partner benefits: **None**

You've just got to love DEC, if for nothing else than for fostering a vibrant lesbian and gay culture, as expressed in all those groups. They have considerable impact on both the gay and the business communities, especially throughout New England—but it's a lot tougher for "people like us" in DEC facilities outside that area—say, in Houston. The former CEO (who founded DEC in 1957 and retired in 1991) was an outspoken advocate of inclusive diversity. Under his encouragement the company developed one of the most comprehensive (and admired) diversity education programs anywhere. But things seem to have stalled at the second-largest computer maker over equal benefits. (Oh, no! They're using the cost argument!) At least, many seem embarrassed by the lack of them. Maybe if all those wonderful groups could band together a bit tighter, the process could be speeded up.

The Walt Disney Company   ▽▽▽

Headquartered: **Burbank, CA**

Other Major Locations: **Florida, California, New York, and worldwide**

Approximate Number of Employees: **50,000**

Rating: **GOOD**

Written policy prohibits discrimination: **Yes, since 1992**

Includes awareness of gay and lesbian issues in training: **Yes, for managers**

Lesbian and gay employee group: **LEAGUE (the company's first employee group, has since fostered others)**

Domestic-partner benefits:

   Access to company events and facilities

The dilemma at Disney (not unique to them, but they think so) is how to square the fact that they're a gay-friendly employer with their squeaky- (I don't use the word lightly) clean image as the icon of American family values. (This could be the subtext for a great animation, no?) So they don't like to talk about it. But they're a lot more diversified these days than Mickey, Tinkerbelle (ahem), and the theme parks. (There are also Touchstone Pictures and Hyperion—EuroDisney is a separate entity.) They must realize they'll never be able to pull off the historical-concept park in Virginia without considerable gay wit and imagination—though don't expect a reenactment of the Stonewall Riots. Disney is a likely candidate for equal benefits in the near future. (Yes, the coveted spousal passes to the Magic Kingdoms are now available to domestic partners. I'm told it's not exactly policy, but anybody who wants them has them.)

Dow Chemical Corp.

$\triangledown$

Headquartered: **Midland, MI**
Other Major Locations: **Texas, Louisiana, and nationwide**
Approximate Number of Employees: **20,000**
Rating: **TRYING**

Written policy prohibits discrimination: **Yes, since 1993**
Includes awareness of gay and lesbian issues in training: **No**
Lesbian and gay employee group: **In formation**
Domestic-partner benefits: **None**

While it may seem like a case of keeping up with DuPont (which, at least in part, it certainly is) credit also belongs to Dow employees brave enough to be out in the rough-and-tumble chemical industry. There's a long way to go here. Lesbian and gay issues are still not accepted as a valid part of the diversity program, which says a lot about attitudes—but the process has begun.

E. I. DuPont de Nemours ▽▽▽

Headquartered: **Wilmington, DE**
Other Major Locations: **Worldwide**
Approximate Number of Employees: **95,000 (125,000 worldwide)**
Rating: **GOOD**

Written policy prohibits discrimination: **Yes, since 1991**
Includes awareness of gay and lesbian issues in training: **Yes**
Lesbian and gay employee group: **BGLAD (Bisexuals, Gays & Lesbians at DuPont)**
Domestic-partner benefits: **None**

A surprising but genuine champ on gay and lesbian issues, DuPont has made considerable effort since the late 1980s to enlist its employees in the process of change and improvement—and to overcome its ancient image as paternalistic, exclusive, and a menace to the environment. That last may take a while (and we can be sure our gay and lesbian colleagues are doing their part) but otherwise change has come relatively fast. Diversity efforts are taken seriously (that is, encouraged from the top) for *all* minorities. Furthermore, the company has recognized (with actual awards) the courage of its lesbian and gay employees. Fair benefits are a likely next step. (By the way, policies, training, and the employee group also cover DuPont's petroleum subsidiary Conoco and its pharmaceutical affiliate DuPont-Merck.)

Eastern Mountain Sports   ▽▽

Headquartered: **Peterborough, NH**
Other Major Locations: **Stores from Maine to Washington, DC, plus Minnesota and Colorado**
Approximate Number of Employees: **1,000**
Rating: **GOOD**

Written policy prohibits discrimination: **Yes, since 1991**
Includes awareness of gay and lesbian issues in training: **Sort of**
Lesbian and gay employee group: **None**
Domestic-partner benefits:

> **Bereavement/sickness leave**

While the rock-ribbed Yankee management of this outdoor clothing and equipment retailer (now a division of the Dutch-owned Amcena Corp.) is said to be getting over its initial shock, lesbian and gay employees applaud efforts at openness and inclusiveness in policy, employee articles, and management's use of language. The company promotes diversity awareness in an individualistic and outdoorsy way, encouraging employees to "examine the layers inside of you" and share the experience. It also sponsors a "Volunteer Day" (gay and lesbian causes included), "life-enhancement days," and best of all, employee "adventure leave" for pursuing those dreams of your choice. Sounds like fun.

Episcopal Diocese of Newark   ▽▽▽▽

Headquartered: **Newark, NJ**
Approximate Number of Employees: **200**
Rating: **GOOD**

———

Written policy prohibits discrimination: **Not written, but
standard practice**
Includes awareness of gay and lesbian issues in training: **Yes,
with homophobia awareness programs and inclusion in diversity and harassment training**
Lesbian and gay employee group: **None**
Domestic-partner benefits:

> **Dental plan**
> **(Health coverage exists in policy since 1992, but Aetna, the
> plan carrier, refused to cover. Negotiations ensued, but
> there's no resolution yet.)**

Whatever theological discussions about the status of gay
men and lesbians may rip through the Episcopal Church
in America, this one diocese, which includes about 130
churches in northern New Jersey, just went ahead and
tried to establish equity for lesbian and gay clergy and
other employees. Not surprisingly, this was the first Episcopal diocese to ordain openly gay priests. One of them
became the first invited to lead a non-gay congregation.
(The rectory he and his partner share is pretty nice too.)

Federal National Mortgage Association (Fannie Mae) ∨∨∨∨∨

Headquartered: **Washington, DC**
Other Major Locations: **Philadelphia, Atlanta, Dallas, Pasadena, and Chicago**
Approximate Number of Employees: **3,000**
Rating: **EXCELLENT**

Written policy prohibits discrimination: **Yes, since 1992**
Includes awareness of gay and lesbian issues in training: **Yes, a little**
Lesbian and gay employee group: **FLAG (Fannie Mae Lesbians and Gays), said to be the largest of any employee affinity group**
Domestic-partner benefits: **All benefits equal to those for spouse; opposite-sex domestic partners included**

> **Access to company events and facilities**
> **Bereavement/sickness leave**
> **Employee Assistance Program/counseling**
> **Relocation assistance**
> **Health coverage (includes partner's dependents too)**
> **Dental plan (same)**
> **Vision plan**
> **Pension/survivor options**
> **Adoption benefits**
> **Legal insurance**

A company traded on the New York Stock Exchange, Fannie Mae isn't a government agency (as many think), although the President appoints some board members and Congress has some oversight responsibilities (fortunately not including employment practices). Its business is to keep mortgage money flowing around the country, but it's also taken an interest in the "high moral ground" as an employer. Witness its reputation as a great employer for women and, more recently, for lesbians and gay men. The benefits plan is one of the best around and fully equal. While its educational efforts in-house about gay and lesbian issues could be more forthright, a new initiative is planned for 1994. Non-gay employees, as well as top management, are supportive. To them, it's all about taking a realistic view of "family," like better child care. They get extra points for that.

Frame Technology Corp. ▽▽▽

Headquartered: **San Jose, CA**
Approximate Number of Employees: **325 (425 worldwide)**
Rating: **GOOD?**

Written policy prohibits discrimination: **Not sure**
Includes awareness of gay and lesbian issues in training: **No**
Lesbian and gay employee group: **None**
Domestic-partner benefits:

Health coverage
Dental plan

Lesbian and gay employees are known to exist through the company E-mail—but that seems to be the extent of visibility. Surprising for a Silicon Valley software maker, no? It seems that new management—described carefully as "more conservative"—took over in 1993. Seems a lot of senior people left. The existing domestic-partner health and dental benefits were inherited. They remain, and I don't want to sound ungrateful, but, hey, something uncomfortable is happening here.

Gannett Co., Inc. ▽▽▽

Headquartered: **Arlington, VA**
Other Major Locations: **Eighty-three newspapers, twelve TV stations, and billboards nationwide**
Approximate Number of Employees: **36,000**
Rating: **GOOD**

Written policy prohibits discrimination: **Yes**
Includes awareness of gay and lesbian issues in training: **Yes**
Lesbian and gay employee group: **Informal only**
Domestic-partner benefits:

> **Bereavement/sickness leave**
> **Relocation assistance (includes job-placement counseling)**

Circumstances vary by location, but the publisher of *USA Today* and the rest is considered a pretty fair employer, certainly on the corporate level. It shows in pretty fair coverage of gay and lesbian issues—most endearingly, with the only syndicated columnist with a specifically lesbian and gay beat: Deb Price, out of—and out at—the *Detroit News.*

Gardener's Supply Co.   ▽▽▽▽▽

Headquartered: **Burlington, VT**
Approximate Number of Employees: **110**
Rating: **EXCELLENT**

Written policy prohibits discrimination: **Yes, since 1990**
Includes awareness of gay and lesbian issues in training: **No formal diversity training, but does state in policy that anti-gay harassment won't be tolerated**
Lesbian and gay employee group: **None**
Domestic-partner benefits: **All benefits offered to spouses are applied equally to employees' domestic partners**

> **Access to company events and facilities**
> **Bereavement/sickness leave**
> **Employee Assistance Program/counseling**
> **Discounts**
> **Dental plan**
> **Health coverage (Insurance carrier won't recognize domestic partners in plan; instead, the company subsidizes the cost of individual plans for uninsured partners.)**

Like its Vermont neighbor Ben & Jerry's, this small catalog house takes pride in its progressive policies—and walks the talk even when insurers won't cooperate. There aren't any openly gay managers near the top, but more than a few working up the ranks, and the overall environment is considered pretty supportive. Maybe it's the cold, clear air up there.

Genentech Inc. ▽▽▽▽

Headquartered: **South San Francisco, CA**
Other Major Locations: **Field offices worldwide**
Approximate Number of Employees: **2,400**
Rating: **GOOD**

Written policy prohibits discrimination: **Yes, since 1991**
Includes awareness of gay and lesbian issues in training: **Yes**
Lesbian and gay employee group: **Gays, Lesbians, Bisexuals & Friends at Genentech**
Domestic-partner benefits: **(in practice, without specific policy)**

> **Access to company events and facilities**
> **Bereavement/sickness leave**
> **Employee Assistance Program/counseling**

Taking pride in the idea that it's not "policy driven," Genentech doesn't have a lot of things written down, but it's managed to create a comfortable environment while pioneering an industry. The leading biotechnology firm, it produces "human pharmaceuticals"—genetically engineered products such as human growth hormone and medications for cystic fibrosis, certain immune disorders, and cleansing blood clots after heart attacks. It also distributes these items free to the needy and the uninsured. As for its own employee benefits, all are undergoing a review process, with equalized benefits a distinct possibility.

General Motors Corp. ▽

Headquartered: **Detroit, MI**

Other Major Locations: **Indiana, Ohio, Wisconsin, Missouri, Georgia, and worldwide**

Approximate Number of Employees: **500,000 (750,000 worldwide)**

Rating: **TRYING**

Written policy prohibits discrimination: **Yes**

Includes awareness of gay and lesbian issues in training: **In process**

Lesbian and gay employee group: **Yes**

Domestic-partner benefits: **None**

Don't get overly excited; it's going to take a long time before every lesbian and gay employee at GM can expect safety, let alone acceptance and equality. But the wheels are turning. With honesty, persistence, and persuasiveness coming out at influential levels, the nation's largest private employer has begun to take a serious look at rampant homophobia, harassment, and discrimination. Gay-inclusive diversity issues have been discussed at board level, and strong messages sent from the CEO. Training programs have been initiated at management level. An employee group, spanning all divisions, management and union, has moved into gear. A lot of education has to take place here, but the company's on the right road. A long way from *Roger and Me.*

Greenpeace International   ∇∇∇∇∇

Headquartered: **Washington, DC**
Approximate Number of Employees: **1,000**
Rating: **EXCELLENT**

Written policy prohibits discrimination: **Yes, since 1993**
Includes awareness of gay and lesbian issues in training: **Yes (when it does training)**
Lesbian and gay employee group: **None (Who has time?)**
Domestic-partner benefits:

> **Bereavement/sickness leave**
> **Employee Assistance Program/counseling**
> **Discounts**
> **Health coverage**
> **Dental plan**
> **Pension plan allows any designated beneficiary**

Despite the large numbers of lesbians and gay men who work in the environmental movement, this is the only environmental group to offer full, fair benefits. Then again, you don't get much else when you work nonprofit, except the satisfaction. I've heard there are gay dolphins, and probably whales, but I'm sure that makes no difference in saving them.

Harley Davidson Inc. ▽

Headquartered: **Milwaukee, WI**
Other Major Locations: **Pennsylvania, Wisconsin, and Indiana**
Approximate Number of Employees: **5,800**
Rating: **TRYING**

Written policy prohibits discrimination: **Yes, since mid 1980s**
Includes awareness of gay and lesbian issues in training: **In development**
Lesbian and gay employee group: **None**
Domestic-partner benefits: **None**

The corporate philosophy, I was told without a trace of irony, is that "those who work here drive the business." Hopefully, they drive the motorcycles and RVs too. There seems to be a certain appreciation of the, shall we say, affection some members of the lesbian and gay community have for their Harleys. But coming out here must still be a problem: few have. The company says it would recognize an employee group, if anyone asked. It might also talk about benefits (though it has to negotiate its union contracts first). Maybe some gay-inclusive training would rev things up here.

Harvard University ∇∇∇∇∇

Headquartered: **Cambridge, MA**
Approximate Number of Employees: **15,000**
Rating: **EXCELLENT**

Written policy prohibits discrimination: **Yes**
Includes awareness of gay and lesbian issues in training: **Yes**
Lesbian and gay employee group: **Several**
Domestic-partner benefits:

> **Health coverage**
> **Dental plan**

It's said that the nation's premier educational institution was waiting for another university of its class (and its Cambridge neighbor MIT) to take the plunge into offering domestic-partner benefits. MIT jumped first, setting off a major trend. Harvard's benefits went into effect January 1994.

Herman Miller ▽▽▽

Headquartered: **Zeeland, MI**
Other Major Locations: **Georgia, Texas, California, and worldwide**
Approximate Number of Employees: **5,600**
Rating: **GOOD**

The distinguished designer and manufacturer of office furniture has a lot to offer all its employees, and makes many a "best company" list. It deserves recognition here too. The company has a model, gay-inclusive non-discrimination policy, is said to have a superb diversity training program (which also addresses lesbian and gay issues), and one occasionally hears rumors of certain domestic partner benefits. Alas, the company will confirm none of it. How much of this is connected with the famed religious conservatism of its western Michigan home, I can't say, but we congratulate the company for what it seems to have accomplished.

Hewlett-Packard Co. ▽▽▽

Headquartered: **Palo Alto, CA**
Other Major Locations: **Colorado, Idaho, Oregon, Massachu-
setts, and throughout California**
Approximate Number of Employees: **57,000 (96,000 world-
wide)**
Rating: **GOOD**

Written policy prohibits discrimination: **Yes, since 1992**
Includes awareness of gay and lesbian issues in training: **Yes**
Lesbian and gay employee group: **Just starting up**
Domestic-partner benefits: **None official**

The CEO talks repeatedly about diversity being a "business essential," but the equipment manufacturer (an
early star in many "quality of life" issues) hasn't caught
on quickly to what its neighboring computer and software makers (which feed an awful lot through H-P print-
ers) know about the advantages of being gay-friendly.
Benefits such as bereavement leave on the death of a
partner are known to exist but are administered on a
case-by-case basis. That means on each supervisor's discretion, which is always a risky mixed bag. Change is
coming. But where's the resistance dug in?

HBO/Time-Warner Inc. ▽▽▽▽▽

Headquartered: **New York, NY**
Approximate Number of Employees: **1,000 (HBO)**
Rating: **EXCELLENT**

Written policy prohibits discrimination: **Yes, as of 1993**
Includes awareness of gay and lesbian issues in training: **Yes**
Lesbian and gay employee group: **Time-Warner Lesbian & Gay Task Force**
Domestic-partner benefits:

> **Bereavement/sickness leave**
> **Employee Assistance Program/counseling**
> **Relocation assistance**
> **Health coverage**
> **Dental plan**

Home Box Office, the premium cable source for movies, comedy, and a variety of other entertainments (including its own brave—if somewhat watered-down—production of *And the Band Played On*), has taken the undisputed lead as the gay-friendly subsidary of the vast and complicated Time-Warner media empire. (That's why it's singled out here.) Its sibling subsidiary, the Burbank, CA–based Warner Brothers, followed the script for full benefits, and in late 1993, so did Time-Warner corporate. The allegedly slow-to-change publishing division Time Inc., joined in early 1994. Corporate-wide, there is a non-discrimination policy, and some spectacular diversity education extravaganzas, featuring of course some of Time-Warner's own out talent (like k. d. lang). In fact, the company may even start its own gay magazine. Coincidence?

IDS Financial Services Inc.   ▽▽▽▽

Headquartered: **Minneapolis, MN**
Other Major Locations: **Offices nationwide**
Approximate Number of Employees: **15,000**
Rating: **GOOD**

Written policy prohibits discrimination: **Yes ("for a long time")**
Includes awareness of gay and lesbian issues in training: **Yes, prominently**
Lesbian and gay employee group: **GLEN (Gay & Lesbian Employee Network)**
Domestic-partner benefits: **Under consideration**

Now, this is a company with good attitude. It walks the talk on diversity, it mentors and funds GLEN (including an annual "allowance" for community giving), as it does other employee groups, and it was able to recognize the advantages when openly gay and lesbian financial planners recently started developing financial plans geared to same-sex couples. (Okay, so that last moneymaker really began to change attitudes.) The drawback is that IDS has been owned by American Express since 1986, which doesn't have much of a reputation for responding to mere mortals, let alone lesbian and gay employees. Despite the fact that IDS is AmEx's most profitable arm, the urge to bring all down to the parent's level is expected to put a damper on more equalized benefits. The bright spot is that more IDS executives are being promoted into AmEx headquarters. Let's see what they can do.

International Business Machines Corp. (IBM) ▽

Headquartered: **Armonk, NY**
Other Major Locations: **Worldwide**
Approximate Number of Employees: **150,000**
Rating: **TRYING**

Written policy prohibits discrimination: **Yes, since 1974**
Includes awareness of gay and lesbian issues in training: **Yes, since 1989; mandatory (IBM is so proud of its diversity training program that it has packaged it for sale to other companies.)**
Lesbian and gay employee group: **None (No employee groups are recognized.)**
Domestic-partner benefits:

> **Access to company events**
> **Pension plan permits any designated beneficiary**

Would you have expected IBM on this list? I didn't. Its classic reputation for cookie-cutter conformity clashes with the stated "company value" of "respect for the individual." Its paranoia about unions (thus its hostility to any employee group) makes one wonder about just how responsive to employees it could be. Compared to its competitors and cooperators in the computer field, its gay-friendly benefits are barely tokens. It explains that it "couldn't expand benefits while cutting back on others" since employees must now contribute for the first time. It misses the point about fairness and equality. Still, compared to most other companies, it's not so bad. IBM is in transition, and a lot of gay employees, managers, and even directors are helping to guide that. They're trying. There could be some interesting opportunities here.

Kaiser-Permanente ▽▽▽

Headquartered: **Oakland, CA**
Other Major Locations: **Throughout California**
Approximate Number of Employees: **80,000**
Rating: **GOOD**

Written policy prohibits discrimination: **Yes, date varies by region (Oakland adopted this clause in 1985.)**
Includes awareness of gay and lesbian issues in training: **Yes, in all regions**
Lesbian and gay employee group: **Yes, but not in all regions**
Domestic-partner benefits: **None**

The massive health maintenance organization is noted for its extensive diversity training program. Management is considered very supportive of lesbian and gay employees. (Other issues vary according to the semiautonomous nature of the company's various "regions.") Employees don't have any gay-friendly benefits, and don't expect to get easy coverage for your partner if you're a customer, either. Kaiser has been reluctant, even for big clients. But it's learning.

Kiwi Airlines ▽▽

Headquartered: **Newark, NJ**
Other Major Locations: **Chicago, Orlando, Tampa, West Palm Beach, and San Juan**
Approximate Number of Employees: **630**
Rating: **TRYING**

Written policy prohibits discrimination: **In process**
Includes awareness of gay and lesbian issues in training: **No training**
Lesbian and gay employee group: **None**
Domestic-partner benefits:

> **Bereavement/sickness leave**
> **Discounts**

Since it was founded only in late 1992, this airline doesn't have much policy in place yet. (It was started by pilots and other employees, mostly from Eastern Airlines before it was gutted and sold for scrap—they considered themselves grounded birds, thus the odd name.) Most employees are also shareholders and have the idea of creating an airline "the way it should be." That included, from the beginning, a fresh look at discount flying privileges—one of the most coveted of airline benefits. Instead of the traditional, strict definition of "immediate family only"—a disadvantage to anyone without the legalities— Kiwi employees can designate any six people as their "family." Kiwi deserves credit for that, expecially in the notably ungay-friendly airline industry. We hope it continues the process. (Note: I'm told it's nearly impossible to get a job here without ten years of airline experience. And you'd better enjoy the experience of a start-up venture.)

Eastman Kodak Co.   ▽▽▽

Headquartered: **Rochester, NY**
Other Major Locations: **California, Colorado, and worldwide**
Approximate Number of Employees: **48,000 (132,000 world-wide)**
Rating: **GOOD**

Written policy prohibits discrimination: **Yes, since mid-1980s**
Includes awareness of gay and lesbian issues in training: **Yes**
Lesbian and gay employee group: **Lambda**
Domestic-partner benefits:

Bereavement/sick-care leave
Relocation assistance

This company *hates* publicity, but for buttoned-down corporate Rochester, Kodak has been remarkably receptive to lesbian and gay concerns—which is partly a tribute to the careful, buttoned-down approach of its employee group. Kodak even allows them to hold a "Gayla" at the Eastman House. That's recognition. It may not be picture-perfect here, but there's a good dialogue developing. Let's hope that can continue—the new chief is the former head of (uh-oh) Motorola. In April 1993, Kodak weathered a zany fundamentalist attempt at a boycott: formal recognition of Lambda was equated with support for child molesting. Despite its fears of the spotlight, Kodak didn't budge. Keep sending those UPC codes from their film packaging, with a note of thanks. (You don't have to mention biblical injunctions against "graven images.")

Labor Unions

While not large employers themselves, a growing number of labor unions have adopted non-discrimination policies, recognized gay and lesbian caucuses, sponsored gay-awareness programs, and advocated for (and won) domestic-partner benefits for their members in various companies. Among those unions, working nationally or through various locals, are:

AFL-CIO
American Federation of State, County, and Municipal Workers (AFSCME)
American Federation of Teachers
American Guild of Musical Artists
American Postal Workers Union
Boston Hotel Workers Union
Communications Workers of America (CWA)
International Brotherhood of Teamsters
National Treasury Employees Unions
Oil, Chemical, and Atomic Workers
Screenwriters Guild
Services Employees International Union (SEIU)
United Auto Workers (UAW)
United Food and Commercial Workers

An invaluable source for information about union assistance on gay and lesbian issues is The Lesbian and Gay Labor Network, P.O. Box 1159, Stuyvesant Station, New York, NY 10009

Levi Strauss & Co.   ▽▽▽▽▽

Headquartered: **San Francisco, CA**
Other Major Locations: **Georgia, Texas, New Mexico, and worldwide**
Approximate Number of Employees: **23,000**
Rating: **EXCELLENT**

Written policy prohibits discrimination: **Yes, since early 1970s**
Includes awareness of gay and lesbian issues in training: **Yes**
Lesbian and gay employee group: **Yes**
Domestic-partner benefits:

> **Access to company events and facilities**
> **Bereavement/sickness leave**
> **Employee Assistance Program/counseling**
> **Discounts**
> **Relocation assistance**
> **Health coverage**
> **Dental plan**

The company that everyone immediately thinks of when the term "gay-friendly" is mentioned, Levi Strauss could almost be considered as an extended part of the lesbian and gay community—although that makes many executives who are out cringe for fear of typecasting. It excels in the treatment of its employees. It supports numerous community endeavors. It wouldn't support the Boy Scouts when they insisted on anti-gay discrimination. Its non-gay former president is also one of the most eloquent and tireless spokespersons on AIDS awareness in the workplace. The lesbian and gay coommunity, in return, has been one of the most loyal groups of buyers of 501s, Dockers, and the rest of the clothing line. If there's a flaw anywhere, it's the question about gay and lesbian employees outside the Bay Area. Has anyone found them yet?

Los Angeles Times

Headquartered: **Los Angeles, CA**
Other Major Locations: **Bureaus worldwide**
Approximate Number of Employees: **8,000**
Rating: **GOOD**

Written policy prohibits discrimination: **Yes, since 1990**
Includes awareness of gay and lesbian issues in training: **Yes**
Lesbian and gay employee group: **LA Times Gay & Lesbian Caucus**
Domestic-partner benefits: **None**

Like most major newspapers, the Los Angeles *Times* has had to get through a lot of old journalistic prejudice just to do its job right in reporting the news, especially about lesbian and gay issues. Gay and lesbian reporters have taken much of the initiative here. The newsroom is reported to be more comfortable. (This is not necessarily true of the *Times*'s parent company, Times-Mirror.) Diversity training, formerly required only of editors, is now being extended to all employees. And the new stylebook, released in late 1993 to much derision, is an admirable standard for the sensitivities diversity needs to address. (I'm not sure about "Dutch treat" being offensive but, yes, "gay" is preferable to "homosexual," thank you.) As for equalized benefits, I hear that LA is waiting for its New York counterpart to take the first step. But *The New York Times*, on reading, still seems to prefer "homosexual" to "gay."

Lotus Development Corp.   ▽▽▽▽▽

Headquartered: **Cambridge, MA**
Other Major Locations: **Worldwide**
Approximate Number of Employees: **3,200**
Rating: **EXCELLENT**

Written policy prohibits discrimination: **Yes**
Includes awareness of gay and lesbian issues in training: **Yes**
Lesbian and gay employee group: **Yes**
Domestic-partner benefits:

Access to company events and facilities
Bereavement/sickness leave
Employee Assistance Program/counseling
Relocation assistance
Health coverage
Dental plan

Lotus put the national spotlight on health coverage for domestic partners in September 1991 when it became the first publicly held company to offer the benefit to its gay and lesbian employees. (There had been other and larger employers, but none that was publicly traded, and none that had made it a specifically gay benefit.) The software maker took a lot of flak for this—not from employees or shareholders, but from the media. Happily, Lotus also set off a virtual stampede among other high-tech companies eagerly competing for talent to match its benefits package. Lotus also (inadvertently, I suppose) changed the standard for gay-friendly companies overnight, with itself at the top of the list.

Massachusetts Institute
of Technology (MIT)

▽▽▽▽▽

Headquartered: **Cambridge, MA**
Approximate Number of Employees: **8,000**
Rating: **EXCELLENT**

Written policy prohibits discrimination: **Yes, since 1988**
Includes awareness of gay and lesbian issues in training: **Yes**
Lesbian and gay employee group: **GaBLES (Gay, Bisexual &
    Lesbian Employees & Students)**
Domestic-partner benefits:

> **Access to company events and facilities**
> **Bereavement/sickness leave**
> **Employee Assistance Program/counseling**
> **Health coverage**
> **Dental plan**

High-technology companies often cite lessons learned at
MIT as the basis for their own diversity philosophies: if
you're smart enough and good enough to do the job,
then who cares who you are? Well, that may not have all
the niceties of modern diversity practice, but it does reveal some of the competitiveness inherent in the field.
Whether you're talking Silicon Valley or education.

MCA, Inc. ▽▽▽▽▽

Headquartered: **Universal City, CA**
Other Major Locations: **New York City and worldwide**
Approximate Number of Employees: **16,000**
Rating: **EXCELLENT**

Written policy prohibits discrimination: **Yes, since 1992**
Includes awareness of gay and lesbian issues in training: **Yes;
    also sponsors special homophobia awareness and AIDS-
    education programs**
Lesbian and gay employee group: **None**
Domestic-partner benefits:

**Health coverage
Dental plan
Vision plan
Pension/survivor benefits (in process)**

Suddenly, amid angry protests about Hollywood depictions of lesbian and gay characters (remember *Basic Instinct*?), this media conglomerate (Universal Pictures, Putnam Publishing, various television and recording interests) burst forth with some of the gay-friendliest policies in town. It triggered a complete reversal of attitude in the entertainment industry, once one of the most homophobic, even though it was filled with us (remember Rock Hudson?). Now MCA works hand-in-hand with LA activists, and even its Japanese owner (megacorporation Matsushita) doesn't seem to mind. You never hear much from the employees themselves, but, hey, it can't hurt the marketing. Its CEO was quoted as saying, "In a recession, no one can afford to be homophobic." Anyway, you have to love the company for issuing the whole Mae West library on videotape.

Methodist Hospital of Indianapolis ▽▽

Headquartered: **Indianapolis, IN**
Approximate Number of Employees: **6,000**
Rating: **TRYING**

Written policy prohibits discrimination: **Yes, since early 1980s**
Includes awareness of gay and lesbian issues in training: **Yes**
Lesbian and gay employee group: **None**
Domestic-partner benefits: **None**

Invisibility is a big issue here among lesbian and gay employees, and that's not helped by hostility among some individuals (including at the board of directors level) who use the hospital's traditional religious affiliation as an excuse. But the culture is changing: a gay and lesbian panel and a video recently incorporated into diversity training were well-received, and the hospital (which includes satellite facilities throughout the area) has become the chief sponsor of the Indianapolis AIDS Walk. Logical, of course, but worthy of extra credit in Quayle country.

Microsoft Corp. ▽▽▽▽▽

Headquartered: **Redmond, WA**
Approximate Number of Employees: **12,000**
Rating: **EXCELLENT**

Written policy prohibits discrimination: **Yes, since 1990**
Includes awareness of gay and lesbian issues in training: **Yes**
Lesbian and gay employee group: **GLEAM (Gay, Lesbian & Bi-sexual Employees at Microsoft)**
Domestic-partner benefits:

> **Bereavement/sickness leave**
> **Health coverage**
> **Dental plan**

You work very hard here to earn your stock and get very rich (although never as rich as the chairman). It's amazing you have any time for a personal life at all. Everybody is so busy making best-selling software that niceties such as diversity or gay and lesbian issues tend to get overlooked. So the company isn't exactly a leader. But it does deliver. Lesbian and gay employees seem pretty content here. By their Word.

Milbank, Tweed, Hadley, & McCloy

ᐯᐯᐯᐯᐯ

Headquartered: **New York, NY**
Other Major Locations: **Worldwide**
Approximate Number of Employees: **1,000**
Rating: **EXCELLENT**

Written policy prohibits discrimination: **Yes, since 1990**
Includes awareness of gay and lesbian issues in training: **Yes (good program too)**
Lesbian and gay employee group: **Informal (some members serve on firm's diversity committee)**
Domestic-partner benefits:

> **Employee Assistance Program/counseling**
> **Health coverage**
> **Dental plan**

A corporate, Wall Street law firm that's gay-friendly might surprise some, but it likes to think of itself as "user-friendly," and the large number of lesbian and gay attorneys here are making the most of it. (It seems odd that the firm lacks a bereavement leave policy, but I'm told it's administered on a case-by-case basis. C'mon, folks, you know the value of the written word. Put it on paper.)

Minnesota Communications Group

∇∇∇∇∇

Headquartered: **St. Paul, MN**
Approximate Number of Employees: **800**
Rating: **EXCELLENT**

Written policy prohibits discrimination: **Yes, since 1989**
Includes awareness of gay and lesbian issues in training: **No training**
Lesbian and gay employee group: **Informal only**
Domestic-partner benefits:

> **Access to company events and facilities**
> **Bereavement/sickness leave**
> **Health coverage**
> **Dental plan**
> **Pension plan allows named beneficiary**

The nonprofit side of this company (Minnesota Public Radio) produces highly successful radio programs (*A Prairie Home Companion*), while the for-profit side handles merchandising (from tapes to T-shirts). This close to Lake Wobegon, you couldn't ask for a friendlier or more open environment. Whatever policies helpful to gay and lesbian employees aren't written exist in spirit. If you need it, just ask. (By the way, the employees of American Public Radio, a smaller, separate but related organization, are covered under the same benefits plan.)

Minnesota Mining & Manufacturing Co. (3M Corp.) ▽▽

Headquartered: **St. Paul, MN**
Other Major Locations: **Worldwide**
Approximate Number of Employees: **49,000 (87,000 world-wide)**
Rating: **GOOD**

Written policy prohibits discrimination: **Yes, since 1992**
Includes awareness of gay and lesbian issues in training: **Yes**
Lesbian and gay employee group: **3M PLUS (People Like Us)**
Domestic-partner benefits: **None**

The maker of Scotch tape (among other chemicals and products) puts a lot of value on listening to its employees. Legend has it that the ubiquitous Post-it notes came about that way—invented by an employee whose job wasn't to invent. On the gay side, according to stories, it wasn't an easy start. (It's almost funny how often you hear insiders say, "You know, this is a *very* conservative company.") Still, once lesbian and gay employees presented their concerns, management acted. When sexual orientation was added to the company's affirmative action policy, it was explained in a feature article in the employee magazine, emphasizing how the new rule was essential to 3M's Human Resource Principles, consistent with "the respect and dignity that each employee is entitled to," and everyone's responsibility to adhere to. Letters, pro and con, flew for months. But visibility, comfort, and progress continue to grow. Obviously, this is the result of lesbian and gay employees sticking together and sticking up for themselves.

Montefiore Medical Center   ▽▽▽▽▽

Headquartered: **Bronx, NY**
Approximate Number of Employees: **10,000**
Rating: **EXCELLENT**

Written policy prohibits discrimination: **Yes, since 1989**
Includes awareness of gay and lesbian issues in training: **Yes**
(also addresses homophobia in AIDS-awareness program for all employees)
Lesbian and gay employee group: **None is registered**
Domestic-partner benefits: **Apply only to about 3,500 non-union employees (including management, doctors, scientists, secretaries, and security guards) (Nurses and other unionized medical workers will need to negotiate new contracts.)**

   Access to company events and facilities
   Bereavement/sickness leave
   Employee Assistance Program/counseling
   Health coverage

Montefiore, long considered a gay-friendly environment within the medical field, became the pioneer in the health-care industry by offering domestic-partner health coverage in 1991. Its was also the first policy anywhere to specify "same-sex" couples only (surprising many who were promoting domestic-partner benefits regardless of sexual orientation). Their reasoning? Lesbians and gay men are specifically *prohibited* from marrying and thus have no other options. The fairness may be questionable, but the policy is nevertheless gay-friendly.

Morrison & Foerster ▽▽▽▽▽

Headquartered: **San Francisco, CA**
Other Major Locations: **Seattle, Denver, Los Angeles, New York, and Washington, DC**
Approximate Number of Employees: **1,600**
Rating: **EXCELLENT**

Written policy prohibits discrimination: **Yes, since the 1970s**
Includes awareness of gay and lesbian issues in training: **Yes**
Lesbian and gay employee group: **Yes**
Domestic-partner benefits:

> **Access to company events and facilities**
> **Bereavement/sickness leave**
> **Employee Assistance Program/counseling**
> **Health coverage subsidy**
> **Dental plan**
> **Vision plan**

The largest law firm in San Francisco has a progressive reputation and makes many "best" lists. It offers advantages in flextime, elder care, family leave, and for working parents. However, its attempts to offer health coverage to same-sex partners were rebuffed by the usual culprit: its insurance carrier. MoFo's appreciated response has been to instead provide a cash subsidy (equal to what it pays in for spouses) for a partner's individual plan. The same deal applies to a partner's children. If that's not enough, the firm deserves credit for taking early leadership in the development of policy toward HIV and for pro bono legal work within the lesbian and gay community. Thanks.

Municipal Government

Although they don't operate on exactly the same premises as private companies, local governments are concerned about the quality and well-being of their employees (as well as the opinions of their constituents). Those listed below have non-discrimination policies, lesbian and gay employee groups, some awareness training, and domestic-partner benefits that at least include health coverage:

Austin, TX
Berkeley, CA
Boston, MA
Cambridge, MA
East Lansing, MI
Los Angeles, CA
Minneapolis, MN
New York, NY
Portland, OR
San Francisco, CA
Santa Cruz, CA
Seattle, WA
Washington, DC
West Hollywood, CA

Numerous other municipalities and related agencies offer at least non-discrimination policies (call yours to ask!) and employee groups can be found in places as unlikely as the Port Authority of New York and New Jersey or the Chicago Transit Authority.

Nabisco Foods Group/RJR Nabisco ▽

Headquartered: **East Hanover, NJ**
Other Major Locations: **Georgia, Illinois, California, Minnesota, Pennsylvania, North Carolina**
Approximate Number of Employees: **25,000**
Rating: **TRYING**

Written policy prohibits discrimination: **Yes**
Includes awareness of gay and lesbian issues in training: **Yes**
Lesbian and gay employee group: **Yes**
Domestic-partner benefits: **None**

Perhaps the best known of the megacorporations created during the mergers-and-acquisitions mania of the 1980s (remember *Barbarians at the Gate*?), RJR Nabisco has three distinct cultures: Nabisco Foods, R.J. Reynolds Tobacco, and the corporate entity that holds them together. For this list, North Carolina–based Reynolds is excluded— not to appease the antismoking set, but because it has nothing to recommend itself as a workplace for lesbians and gay men. Nabisco has been making gradual progress under courageous leadership—inclusive diversity programs were scheduled to begin in 1994—but the process should accelerate with its new employee group. Actually, RJRN corporate (with only two hundred employees, based in Manhattan) has been providing strong if cautious leadership, with encouragement of lesbian and gay visibility, active involvement in AIDS-awareness groups, sponsorship of the AIDS Quilt (displayed at headquarters), community funding, and otherwise keeping gay and lesbian issues on the agenda. One to watch.

National Organization for Women (NOW)

∨∨∨∨∨

Headquartered: **Washington, DC**
Approximate Number of Employees: **30**
Rating: **EXCELLENT**

Written policy prohibits discrimination: **Yes, since 1970**
(They don't seem to come any earlier than this.)
Includes awareness of gay and lesbian issues in training: **Yes**
(There's also a full-time staff person who works on lesbian-rights issues.)
Lesbian and gay employee group: **None**
Domestic-partner benefits:

> **Access to company events and facilities**
> **Bereavement/sickness leave**
> **Health coverage**
> **Dental plan**

It would have been a disappointment *not* to see NOW on this list, given the long history of support by the women's movement for lesbian *and* gay issues (hopefully reciprocated). Since the information here refers to only the national organization (there are also more than seven hundred chapters nationwide), NOW proves that any employer—nonprofit or for profit—with a small staff can still deliver the full gay-friendly package. If she wants to.

National Public Radio (NPR) ∨∨∨∨∨

Headquartered: **Washington, DC**
Other Major Locations: **Bureaus in New York, Chicago, and Los Angeles**
Approximate Number of Employees: **400**
Rating: **EXCELLENT**

Written policy prohibits discrimination: **Yes**
Includes awareness of gay and lesbian issues in training: **Yes**
Lesbian and gay employee group: **Yes, and "very active"**
Domestic-partner benefits:

> **Access to company events and facilities**
> **Bereavement/sickness leave**
> **Relocation assistance**
> **Health coverage**
> **Dental plan**
> **Pension plan permits any designated beneficiary**

Probably the most respected source for news reporting (as well as entertainment programming) in the nation, NPR reported in 1981 about a "mysterious disease" affecting gay men long before anyone else in the news caught on. This was probably because it was doing its job without prejudice. NPR's employment practices are consistent—among the best.

New York University   ▽▽▽▽

Headquartered: **New York, NY**
Approximate Number of Employees: **12,000**
Rating: **GOOD**

Written policy prohibits discrimination: **Yes**
Includes awareness of gay and lesbian issues in training: **Not specifically**
Lesbian and gay employee group: **Ad hoc only**
Domestic-partner benefits: **In process**

As the most powerful institutional presence in Greenwich Village, NYU finds itself living amid an ongoing course in diversity—with a notable lesbian and gay presence. Simultaneously, it has been aggressively courting the image of the most prestigious academic venue in New York, if not beyond. A nationally competitive package of domestic-partner benefits went into effect May 1994.

NeXT Computer Inc. ▽▽▽▽

Headquartered: **Redwood City, CA**
Approximate Number of Employees: **240**
Rating: **GOOD**

Written policy prohibits discrimination: **Yes, since 1985**
Includes awareness of gay and lesbian issues in training: **No
    diversity training**
Lesbian and gay employee group: **Informal, just starting up**
Domestic-partner benefits:

**Access to company events and facilities
Bereavement/sickness leave**

The intention was, from its very founding in 1985, that
software-maker NeXT would have equal benefits for all
employees, regardless of sexual orientation. Its proposed
domestic-partner health plan, in 1986, would have been
among the first in the nation. (It says it wasn't even aware
of *The Village Voice's* innovation.) But its insurance carrier
refused to cover same-sex couples, openly admitting it
didn't want to deal with the possibility of AIDS. Nowa-
days that would result in an instantaneous lawsuit. The
unique result is that NeXT offers domestic-partner benefits, but only to unmarried couples of the *opposite* sex.
Renegotiations (with the same carrier) are scheduled for
1994. Hopefully, NeXT will do better next time.

Oracle Corp. ▽▽▽▽▽

Headquartered: **Redwood Shores, CA**
Other Major Locations: **Bethesda, MD, and worldwide**
Approximate Number of Employees: **6,000 (10,600 worldwide)**
Rating: **EXCELLENT**

Written policy prohibits discrimination: **Yes, since 1986**
Includes awareness of gay and lesbian issues in training: **Yes**
Lesbian and gay employee group: **Lambda Club**
Domestic-partner benefits:

> **Access to company events and facilities**
> **Bereavement/sickness leave**
> **Employee Assistance Program/counseling**
> **Relocation assistance**
> **Health coverage**
> **Dental plan**
> **Vision plan**

The largest supplier of information-management software (some of it familiar in the human resources department) could easily provide the model for any gay-friendly, employee-responsive corporation of the future. Oracle differs from many of its high-tech neighbors in that its health, dental, and vision coverage are for same-sex couples only.

Orrick, Herrington & Sutcliffe   ▽▽▽▽▽

Headquartered: **San Francisco, CA**
Other Major Locations: **New York, Washington, Los Angeles, and Sacramento**
Approximate Number of Employees: **750**
Rating: **EXCELLENT**

Written policy prohibits discrimination: **Yes**
Includes awareness of gay and lesbian issues in training: **No training (considers the environment of San Francisco sufficient)**
Lesbian and gay employee group: **Informal only**
Domestic-partner benefits:

> **Bereavement/sickness leave**
> **Employee Assistance Program/counseling**
> **Health coverage**
> **Dental plan**
> **Vision plan**

As one of the largest law firms dealing with public finance in San Francisco (and elsewhere), this employer has a fairly high political profile in several gay-friendly jurisdictions. So it hasn't hurt to have some extra political appeal. The firm says it's also in the process of redefining its whole stance on "family." One peculiarity: At the insistence of its insurance carrier, domestic partners are required to be legally registered in some city that provides a domestic partner registry. Luckily for employees, San Francisco, New York, Washington, DC, and Los Angeles offer that option, but folks in Sacramento would seem to be inconvenienced. Do they check marriage licenses too?

Pacific Gas & Electric Co.

Headquartered: **San Francisco, CA**
Other Major Locations: **Throughout California**
Approximate Number of Employees: **24,000**
Rating: **GOOD**

Written policy prohibits discrimination: **Yes, since 1982**
Includes awareness of gay and lesbian issues in training: **Yes, for all employees**
Lesbian and gay employee group: **PG&E GLBSA**
Domestic-partner benefits:

> **Access to company events and facilities**
> **Bereavement/sickness leave**
> **Employee Assistance Program/Counseling**
> **Relocation assistance**

For the utility that covers forty-eight counties in California, there's been a lot of learning going on. More than a few San Franciscans offer stories of discrimination suits at PG&E, but the company has a good record in giving to various AIDS causes. There's a learning curve involved, certainly. Today, PG&E flaunts its gay, lesbian, and bisexual employee group (one of the few places where management and union members meet in common cause), as well as how the human resources department is undertaking a study of gay issues with recommendations (benefits maybe?) due in 1994.

Pitney Bowes ▽

Headquartered: **Stamford, CT**
Other Major Locations: **Nationwide**
Approximate Number of Employees: **29,000**
Rating: **TRYING**

Written policy prohibits discrimination: **Yes, since 1991**
Includes awareness of gay and lesbian issues in training: **Yes (but just getting started)**
Lesbian and gay employee group: **None**
Domestic-partner benefits: **None**

The folks who make the postage meters (and a lot of other office equipment) have a good record on minority issues, but gay-inclusiveness is a new discovery for them. The corporate diversity people are enthusiastic, and it's said that upper management is supportive, but the message seems slow trickling down. Why are so many employees afraid to come out, especially as you get farther from headquarters? Even vendors feel the chill: an artist who designed a diversity poster for Pitney Bowes was asked by his boss (a consultant to Pitney Bowes) to remove a pink triangle. How's that for a mixed message? There's potential here, but this envelope needs to be pushed.

Planned Parenthood ∇∇∇∇∇

Headquartered: **New York, NY**
Approximate Number of Employees: **200**
Rating: **EXCELLENT**

Written policy prohibits discrimination: **Yes**
Includes awareness of gay and lesbian issues in train-
ing: **Yes; mandatory**
Lesbian and gay employee group: **Lesbian, Gay & Bisexual
Caucus**
Domestic-partner benefits:

**Access to company events and facilities
Bereavement/sickness leave
Employee Assistance Program/counseling
Health coverage
Dental plan**

Certainly not an employer that is likely to be concerned
about backlash (it may be the only group that knows the
ugliness of fundamentalist rage as well as we do),
Planned Parenthood's openly gay managers and employees speak highly of the organization and its leadership. They also recognize their lesbian and gay clientele;
don't forget they do a considerable amount of work in sex
education and the prevention and treatment of sexually
transmitted diseases. And help *our* parenthood, too. Figures and policies here are for the national organization;
regional chapters act independently on employment
issues.

Portland Cable Access   ▽▽▽▽▽

Headquartered: **Portland, OR**
Approximate Number of Employees: **16**
Rating: **EXCELLENT**

Written policy prohibits discrimination: **Yes, since 1983**
Includes awareness of gay and lesbian issues in training: **Yes**
Lesbian and gay employee group: **None**
Domestic-partner benefits:

> **Access to company events and facilities**
> **Bereavement/sickness leave**
> **Health coverage (in policy)**
> **Dental plan**
> **Vision plan**

While many Oregon employers seem to be intimidated by The Troubles (which is how I've begun to think of the chronic, unrelenting efforts of the so-called Oregon Citizens Alliance to encourage fear, hate, and the passage of laws that specifically allow discrimination against gay men and lesbians), this small, independent nonprofit provides a refreshing bright light. Since its purpose is to facilitate use of community cable stations by *all* members of the Portland citizenry, the company puts a lot of stock (and training) into "team building with different people." It's taken a brave stand with its own employee policies too. The catch with partner health coverage is that, while it exists in policy, it hasn't been activated, since no employee has yet requested it and since the company of course can't find an insurance carrier interested in "team building with different people."

Principal Financial Group Inc. ▽▽▽▽▽

Headquartered: **Des Moines, IA**
Approximate Number of Employees: **12,500**
Rating: **EXCELLENT**

Written policy prohibits discrimination: **Yes, since late 1980s**
Includes awareness of gay and lesbian issues in training: **Yes**
Lesbian and gay employee group: **Yes (but it's a secret)**
Domestic-partner benefits: **All**

> **Access to company events and facilities**
> **Bereavement/sickness leave**
> **Employee Assistance Program/counseling**
> **Relocation assistance**
> **Health coverage**
> **Dental plan**

Here's a company that's way ahead of its community and even a lot of its lesbian and gay employees. What started out as a leadership stance in AIDS education (its CEO is a tireless and eloquent messenger to other CEOs, exhorting them to wake up to AIDS issues in the workplace) quickly turned into an examination of gay and lesbian issues within the company, with a remarkable response. All the more admirable for a financial firm. As for the confidentiality of the employee group, the company spokesperson pointed out, "Remember, this is Des Moines." I suppose so.

Procter & Gamble ▽

Headquartered: **Cincinnati, OH**
Other Major Locations: **Worldwide**
Approximate Number of Employees: **106,000**
Rating: **TRYING**

Procter & Gamble has a long-standing reputation as a private, insular world unto itself, but when the Tide and Crisco maker put sexual orientation into its non-discrimination policy in 1992, it made big news—enough to keep things quiet since. Obviously, the process is in the works. Perhaps the Cincinnati environment hasn't helped—with its Ku Klux Klan Christmas cross, its banning of Mapplethorpe photos, and its decision to take sexual orientation out of its municipal non-discrimination laws, just like Colorado. At least P&G, the biggest employer in town, provides some sort of safe haven.

Public Broadcasting System (PBS) ▽▽▽▽▽

Headquartered: **Washington, DC**
Approximate Number of Employees: **350**
Rating: **EXCELLENT**

Written policy prohibits discrimination: **Yes**
Includes awareness of gay and lesbian issues in training: **No training**
Lesbian and gay employee group: **None**
Domestic-partner benefits:

> **Bereavement/sickness leave**
> **Health coverage**

When PBS was asked about diversity training, the reaction was one of incredulity. Apparently, nobody thinks it's necessary here. I suppose there are few other employers who could get away with that. This *is* PBS. Whether that's just political correctness or not, there are openly gay managers in high places (which fundamentalists and congressional foes of funding have been saying for years, anyway) and the benefits are equal. No commercial broadcast network can say the same.

Recreational Equipment Inc. (REI) ▽▽▽

Headquartered: **Kent, WA**
Other Major Locations: **Stores nationwide**
Approximate Number of Employees: **3,500**
Rating: **GOOD**

Written policy prohibits discrimination: **Yes, since late 1970s**
Includes awareness of gay and lesbian issues in training: **Yes**
Lesbian and gay employee group: **Informal only**
Domestic-partner benefits:

> **Bereavement/sickness leave**
> **Discounts**
> **Relocation assistance**

As one of the premier dealers of camping gear and similar butch accoutrements, REI has had to work through concerns about customer perceptions of being too gay-friendly—even though some of upper management are gay themselves. But it has gotten past stereotypes. Maybe it took a good look at just how much of its supplies lesbians and gay men actually buy. Now REI's right with the program. This is a likely candidate for full benefits in the near future.

Schiff, Hardin & Waite   ▽▽▽▽▽

Headquartered: **Chicago, IL**
Other Major Locations: **New York, Washington, DC, Peoria, and Merrillville, IN**
Approximate Number of Employees: **500**
Rating: **EXCELLENT**

Written policy prohibits discrimination: **Yes**
Includes awareness of gay and lesbian issues in training: **No training**
Lesbian and gay employee group: **None**
Domestic-partner benefits:

> **Access to company events and facilities**
> **Bereavement/sickness leave**
> **Employee Assistance Program/counseling**
> **Discounts**
> **Health coverage**
> **Dental plan**
> **Pension plan permits named beneficiary**

As one of the first major Chicago law firms to admit a black partner (no small deal in Chicago), it's not surprising that it would have the first openly gay ones as well. The gay-friendly benefits (one of only two such programs in town) are seen as essential for recruiting. The "soft" benefits aren't written in policy but are part of practice (which can work in an employer of this size, I guess). Health and dental coverage are for same-sex partners only.

Scholastic Inc. ▽▽▽

Headquartered: **New York, NY**
Other Major Locations: **Missouri, and nationwide**
Approximate Number of Employees: **800**
Rating: **GOOD**

Written policy prohibits discrimination: **Yes**
Includes awareness of gay and lesbian issues in training: **Yes**
Lesbian and gay employee group: **GLAS (Gays and Lesbians
 at Scholastic)**
Domestic-partner benefits:

**Employee Assistance Program/counseling
(others under consideration)**

The renowned publisher of children's books and magazines (with emphasis on teens and teachers) has a reputation dating back to the 1950s as a comfortable
environment for lesbian and gay employees, with (gay-
specific) non-discrimination enshrined in its Code of Ethics. While that hasn't translated into an openly gay or
lesbian presence in top management, GLAS (founded in
spring 1993) is optimistic and enthusiastic, even aiming
for greater attention to lesbian and gay teen concerns
(and addressing issues of censorship) in editorial and
other programs. Oddly, the few complaints heard here
are usually about unresponsiveness in diversity training.
What's the problem?

Charles Schwab & Co., Inc.   ▽▽▽▽▽

Headquartered: **San Francisco, CA**
Other Major Locations: **Nationwide**
Approximate Number of Employees: **4,000**
Rating: **EXCELLENT**

Written policy prohibits discrimination: **Yes, since 1989**
Includes awareness of gay and lesbian issues in training: **Yes**
Lesbian and gay employee group: **None**
Domestic-partner benefits: **All**

Access to company events and facilities
Bereavement/sickness leave
Employee Assistance Program/counseling
Relocation assistance
Health coverage
Dental plan
Pension plan has no beneficiary rules

A role model for rattling the closets of Wall Street, this high-profile discount brokerage house has built a sizable business by offering an alternative approach to investors. Then in 1993 it showed there was nothing incompatible about being in the financial industry and recognizing—even treating equally—the contributions of its gay and lesbian members. Schwab also has an impressive record in AIDS awareness.

Joseph E. Seagram & Sons, Inc. ▽▽▽▽

Headquartered: **New York, NY**
Other Major Locations: **Florida, Indiana, and worldwide**
Approximate Number of Employees: **8,500 (17,000 world-
    wide)**
Rating: **GOOD**

Written policy prohibits discrimination: **Yes**
Includes awareness of gay and lesbian issues in training: **Yes**
Lesbian and gay employee group: **None**
Domestic-partner benefits:

   Access to company events and facilities
   Bereavement/sickness leave

Considered a very gay-friendly company by lesbian and
gay employees (whose numbers include some top-level
management), the distiller and beverage maker (it owns
Tropicana) expects to put every one of its employees
through diversity training by the end of 1994. Issues of
sexual orientation figure prominently in the program.
More comprehensive domestic-partner benefits may
come about through its cafeteria plan for benefits. By the
way, Seagram has a prominent reputation for supporting
AIDS organizations and has been taking a growing interest in specifically gay and lesbian causes; it was the first
corporate sponsor of GLAAD (Gay & Lesbian Alliance
Against Defamation).

Seattle City Light Co.   ▽▽▽▽▽

Headquartered: **Seattle, WA**
Other Major Locations: **Northern and eastern Washington**
Approximate Number of Employees: **1,800**
Rating: **EXCELLENT**

Written policy prohibits discrimination: **Yes, since late 1970s**
Includes awareness of gay and lesbian issues in training: **Yes (specific anti-homophobia program in development)**
Lesbian and gay employee group: **SEAGL (Seattle Employee Association of Gays & Lesbians)**
Domestic-partner benefits:

Access to company events and facilities
Bereavement/sickness leave
Health coverage
Dental plan

As the municipally owned utility, Seattle City Light's employees can claim membership in Seattle's lesbian and gay employee organization and enjoy the city's excellent benefits program. What sets City Light ahead of the city is its exceptionally inclusive diversity training program, which it requires for all employees (the city trains only its managers), and the fact that it also sponsors the program far from the relative safety (and political jurisdiction) of the metropolis.

Seattle Times   ∇∇∇

Headquartered: **Seattle, WA**
Approximate Number of Employees: **2,500**
Rating: **EXCELLENT**

Written policy prohibits discrimination: **Yes**
Includes awareness of gay and lesbian issues in training: **Yes, for all employees**
Lesbian and gay employee group: **GALA**
Domestic-partner benefits:

> **Access to company events and facilities (includes child care)**
> **Bereavement/sickness leave**
> **Health coverage**
> **Dental plan**
> **Pension permits named beneficiary**

Priding itself on its goal of a bias-free workplace, the Seattle daily newspaper has a highly evolved program of diversity training, all-inclusive and dealing strongly with issues of all types of harassment. The immediate prompt for adoption of complete domestic-partner benefits in early 1994 was the passage of the federal Family and Medical Leave Act of the previous year. The company asked itself, "What is the definition of a spouse?," and decided that same-sex partners could be an appropriate equation. (Opposite-sex unmarrieds are not included in the policy, which also has a peculiar throwback provision of a six-month waiting period after application.) But the ultimate reasoning was pure business (in its own business, at least): How could it be objective and bias-free in covering the news unless it was objective and bias-free in its own policies? A worthy question, indeed.

Showtime Networks Inc.   ▽▽▽▽▽

Headquartered: **New York, NY**
Approximate Number of Employees: **700**
Rating: **EXCELLENT**

Written policy prohibits discrimination: **Yes ("always")**
Includes awareness of gay and lesbian issues in training: **Yes**
Lesbian and gay employee group: **Informal only**
Domestic-partner benefits:

> **Bereavement/sickness leave**
> **Employee Assistance Program/counseling**
> **Health coverage**
> **Dental plan**

Although now a subsidiary of Viacom, the cable network has its own independent culture with a strong tradition of gay-friendliness. It administers its own (very active) diversity efforts and has a mandatory AIDS-awareness program for managers, plus community volunteer programs. In addition, it gains considerable advantage from being part of Viacom's exceptionally progressive benefits program.

Silicon Graphics   ▽▽▽▽▽

Headquartered: **Mountain View, CA**
Other Major Locations: **Massachusetts, and nationwide**
Approximate Number of Employees: **2,900 (3,800 worldwide)**
Rating: **EXCELLENT**

Written policy prohibits discrimination: **Yes, since 1991**
Includes awareness of gay and lesbian issues in training: **Yes, extensively**
Lesbian and gay employee group: **Lavender Vision**
Domestic-partner benefits:

> **Access to company events and facilities**
> **Bereavement/sickness leave**
> **Employee Assistance Program/counseling**
> **Discounts**
> **Relocation assistance**
> **Health coverage**
> **Dental plan**
> **Vision plan**
> **Adoption benefits**

In terms of gay-friendly companies, they don't come any better than the leading manufacturer of visual computer systems and multimedia servers. (It's surprising that Silicon Graphics doesn't get more credit for its pioneering work.) It's been built into the culture here. Some upper management has to be described as "getting better," but, still, it's "not okay to be homophobic here." The employee group is respected, diversity training is augmented with AIDS-awareness and Gay Pride programs, all benefits are completely equalized, and the company appreciates the value of being sensitive to privacy.

Stanford University ∨∨∨∨∨

Headquartered: **Palo Alto, CA**
Approximate Number of Employees: **9,000**
Rating: **EXCELLENT**

Written policy prohibits discrimination: **Yes**
Includes awareness of gay and lesbian issues in training: **Yes**
Lesbian and gay employee group: **Yes**
Domestic-partner benefits:

> **Access to company events and facilities**
> **Bereavement/sickness leave**
> **Employee Assistance Program/counseling**
> **Discounts**
> **Health coverage**
> **Dental plan**

By the standards for any employer, Stanford excels. In the education industry, it's by far a leader. Its spectacular campus also happens to host the only national, annual conference on lesbian and gay workplace issues.

Starbucks Coffee Co.   ▽▽▽▽

Headquartered: **Seattle, WA**
Other Major Locations: **Stores in Washington, Oregon, Illinois, California, Colorado, and British Columbia**
Approximate Number of Employees: **4,000**
Rating: **EXCELLENT**

Written policy prohibits discrimination: **Yes, since 1991**
Includes awareness of gay and lesbian issues in training: **No**
Lesbian and gay employee group: **None**
Domestic-partner benefits:

> **Access to company events and facilities**
> **Bereavement/sickness leave**
> **Discounts**
> **Health coverage**
> **Dental plan**
> **Vision plan**

Importer, roaster, and retailer of specialty coffees, with coffee stands up and down the coast and as far east as Chicago and Washington, DC, Starbucks is the type of place that thinks of its employees as "partners." But this place delivers. It distributes stock options to all employees who meet basic qualifications (and the stock has been doing very well). Plus it has one of the most generous benefits plans around for everybody. Even part-timers get health coverage. *Latte*, please!   .

Sun Microsystems Inc. $\vee\vee\vee\vee\vee$

Headquartered: **Mountain View, CA**
Other Major Locations: **California and Massachusetts**
Approximate Number of Employees: **9,000 (13,000 world-wide)**
Rating: **EXCELLENT**

Written policy prohibits discrimination: **Yes, since 1989**
Includes awareness of gay and lesbian issues in training: **Yes**
Lesbian and gay employee group: **GLAF (Gays, Lesbians, and Friends) at Sun**
Domestic-partner benefits:

> **Access to company events and facilities**
> **Bereavement/sickness leave**
> **Employee Assistance Program/counseling**
> **Relocation assistance**
> **Health coverage (includes partner's children too)**
> **Dental plan**

The attitude is very business here. Sun doesn't consider itself a leader, except as "the largest vendor of computer workstations, promoting an open environment and more flexibility for the customer." (PR is such a gas.) Community affairs = investment (but it'll match any employee charitable contribution, up to $1,000). The good benefit policies can be selected under the "Sun-flex" cafeteria plan, so every employee gets the same level of investment too.

United States Government (Civil Service)

Once you subtract the Department of Defense and the offices of certain members of Congress, the vast federal bureaucracy deserves a TRYING rating. This isn't just because of the Clinton administration (which has made a few openly gay and lesbian appointments). The process has been going on for years. Now it can be more public. While there seems to be some disagreement about whether or not the Civil Service actually has a non-discrimination policy, there most certainly is a Federal Gay, Lesbian, and Bisexual Employees group (Federal GLOBE) with active chapters in Washington, DC (of course), Boston, Chicago, Dallas, and Los Angeles, with more in formation. Clear statements of non-discrimination do exist at the departments of Agriculture, Transportation, Housing and Urban Development, Health and Human Services, and Justice. Agriculture is probably the most advanced; an impressive report on internal gay and lesbian issues was put together by its Forest Service division in 1992. The Secretary of Transportation has announced an "open recruitment" policy that is gay-inclusive. The Department of Labor is said to be "supportive." The august State Department has endorsed its own gay and lesbian group and is reported to include domestic partners when Foreign Service employees are shipped abroad. This is progress. Despite recent favorable court decisions, you're best advised to avoid the FBI, which is still living out the legacy of J. Edgar, but there are plenty of other options. Then again, you could run for office.

University of Chicago ▽▽▽▽▽

Headquartered: **Chicago, IL**
Approximate Number of Employees: **6,400**
Rating: **EXCELLENT**

Written policy prohibits discrimination: **Yes**
Includes awareness of gay and lesbian issues in training: **Yes**
Lesbian and gay employee group: **Informal**
Domestic-partner benefits:

> **Bereavement/sickness leave**
> **Employee Assistance Program/counseling**
> **Health coverage**
> **Dental plan**

Like the rest of the higher education field, U of C is keeping up with the competitive edge on lesbian and gay benefits—and became the first Chicago employer to do so. But like the rest of Chicago business, it stays sort of quiet about it all. On the tranquil island of Hyde Park, you may have to find your own way on a lot of issues.

University of Minnesota ∇∇∇∇∇

Headquartered: **St. Paul, MN**
Approximate Number of Employees: **17,000**
Rating: **EXCELLENT**

Written policy prohibits discrimination: **Yes ("for many years")**
Includes awareness of gay and lesbian issues in training: **Yes**
Lesbian and gay employee group: **Yes**
Domestic-partner benefits:

Access to company events and facilities
Bereavement/sickness leave
Health coverage subsidy
Dental plan subsidy

Nice to see the Big Ten represented here, no? The gay-friendly environment shouldn't be a surprise, nor that non-discrimination is mandated directly from the board of regents. What really makes Minnesota outstanding is its willingness to deal directly with the benefits issue: when its carrier balked at the idea of covering employees' domestic partners, the university instead offered a cash reimbursement plan (up to $2,500 per year, what it contributes for spouses) to pay toward private coverage.

U.S. West   ∨∨∨∨

Headquartered: **Englewood, CO**
Other Major Locations: **From Minnesota to Arizona to Pacific Northwest, plus worldwide**
Approximate Number of Employees: **60,000**
Rating: **GOOD**

Written policy prohibits discrimination: **Yes**
Includes awareness of gay and lesbian issues in training: **Yes; mandatory (a model)**
Lesbian and gay employee group: **EAGLE**
Domestic-partner benefits:

Bereavement/sickness leave

The Baby Bell for most of the western states is a highly respected leader in all diversity issues, especially those that concern gay and lesbian employees. The credit belongs to a remarkably open-minded CEO and to a visionary (and thorough) "director of pluralism." But it's the overall atmosphere too. When the emergence of EAGLE caused some consternation, other employee groups (women and racial minorities) were its biggest champions. Now EAGLE works with them as an equal (with its own company funding) to create a mandatory three-day diversity program that should be the standard for corporate America. Openly gay management participates fully without fear of a lavender ceiling. And U.S. West was outstanding in its high-profile opposition to Colorado's anti-gay Amendment Two. Even without full benefits (said to be under consideration while the company reexamines its concept of "family"), this is a uniquely comfortable place to work.

Viacom International Inc. ▽▽▽▽▽

Headquartered: **New York, NY**
Other Major Locations: **Nationwide**
Approximate Number of Employees: **5,000**
Rating: **EXCELLENT**

Written policy prohibits discrimination: **Yes**
Includes awareness of gay and lesbian issues in training: **Yes**
Lesbian and gay employee group: **None**
Domestic-partner benefits:

> **Access to company events and facilities**
> **Bereavement/sickness leave**
> **Employee Assistance Program/counseling**
> **Relocation assistance**
> **Health coverage**
> **Dental plan**
> **Adoption benefits**

Circumstances at Viacom vary by division (Showtime, as the one subsidiary, is considered separately), but corporate headquarters sets a strong standard whether you're in the cable, broadcast, publications, video games, interactive TV, or the MTV division. (Paramount was acquired in 1994.) Each has its own approach to diversity programs, with MTV's "Mixed Masters" probably the most original. Yet all share Viacom's exceptionally progressive benefits plan, which takes a hands-on approach to managing and maximizing employee heath care. Its enlightened approach includes no cap on lifetime benefits, payment for experimental AIDS drugs, and flexible guidelines for job performance standards that encourage employees with chronic health problems (like HIV) to keep working if they wish, rather than be forced into disability.

The Village Voice   ▽▽▽▽

Headquartered: **New York, NY**
Approximate Number of Employees: **225**
Rating: **EXCELLENT**

Written policy prohibits discrimination: **Yes, since 1977**
Includes awareness of gay and lesbian issues in training: **No training**
Lesbian and gay employee group: **Yes**
Domestic-partner benefits:

> **Bereavement/sickness leave**
> **Employee Assistance Program/counseling**
> **Health coverage (union only)**
> **Dental plan (union only)**

I suppose *The Village Voice* (or at least Jeff Weinstein) deserves a plaque or something as the originator of equal benefits for domestic partners in 1982, but the benefits are still limited to union staff only. As New York's venerable alternative weekly newspaper (I'm told some mainlanders read it too), the *Voice* claims the standard for liberalism and political correctness. It's another place where diversity training is considered redundant. That might not be to everyone's taste, but bless 'em for taking a stand.

Wells Fargo & Co.   ▽▽

Headquartered: **San Francisco, CA**
Approximate Number of Employees: **16,000**
Rating: **GOOD**

Written policy prohibits discrimination: **Yes, since 1984**
Includes awareness of gay and lesbian issues in training: **Yes**
Lesbian and gay employee group: **Informal only (no groups recognized)**
Domestic-partner benefits:

Bereavement/sickness leave

It's no surprise that Wells Fargo would take advantage of the hapless situation of its local competitor Bank of America regarding gifts to the Boy Scouts. The way some tales have it, Wells Fargo managers actually set up shop on Castro Street to help gay men and lesbians move their accounts. Although Wells Fargo touts a "family definition" for employees that includes domestic partners, this hasn't translated through the full benefits structure. And the company's rather hostile attitude toward all employee groups has to arouse some suspicion. But the bank is quick to point out that it allows employees marching in San Francisco's Gay Freedom Day parade to use its trademark stagecoach.

WGBH ▽▽▽▽▽

Headquartered: **Boston, MA**
Approximate Number of Employees: **900**
Rating: **EXCELLENT**

Written policy prohibits discrimination: **Yes, since early 1980s (also included in union contracts)**
Includes awareness of gay and lesbian issues in training: **Yes**
Lesbian and gay employee group: **Gay & Lesbian Caucus**
Domestic-partner benefits:

> **Bereavement/sickness leave**
> **Employee Assistance Program/counseling**
> **Health coverage**
> **Dental plan**

This membership-supported television and radio station is not only the local affiliate of the Public Broadcast System but also one of its premier production centers. *Nova* and a lot of international coproductions such as *Masterpiece Theatre* bear the WGBH stamp. Lesbians and gay men are visible at just about every level. You may not get paid as much here as at a commercial network, but it's probably a lot more fun.

Working Assets Funding Service ∇∇∇∇∇

Headquartered: **San Francisco, CA**
Approximate Number of Employees: **45**
Rating: **EXCELLENT**

Written policy prohibits discrimination: **Yes, since 1986**
Includes awareness of gay and lesbian issues in train-
   ing: **No training**
Lesbian and gay employee group: **None**
Domestic-partner benefits:

   Health coverage

A small company with a big idea, Working Assets can't
yet offer its employees all the frills others can afford, but
it delivers what it can. The business is a credit card and
a long-distance telephone service for the socially enlightened: a small charge or a percentage of charges is added
and donated to a variety of causes, gay and lesbian as
well as those concerned with the environment, home-
lessness, and reproductive choice. Often cited as one of
the fastest-growing companies in America, this might be
a satisfying one to grow with.

WQED   ▽▽▽▽▽

Headquartered: **Pittsburgh, PA**
Approximate Number of Employees: **160**
Rating: **EXCELLENT**

———

Written policy prohibits discrimination: **Yes, since 1988**
Includes awareness of gay and lesbian issues in training: **Yes**
Lesbian and gay employee group: **None**
Domestic-partner benefits:

> **Access to company events and facilities**
> **Bereavement/sickness leave**
> **Employee Assistance Program/counseling**
> **Health coverage**
> **Dental plan**

This public broadcasting affiliate offers the only domestic-partner benefits in town, and we don't hear much about gay-inclusive diversity training anywhere else either. That's about as pink as Pittsburgh's Golden Triangle gets.

Xerox Corp.

∇

Headquartered: **Stamford, CT**
Other Major Locations: **California, New York, nationwide, and worldwide**
Approximate Number of Employees: **56,000 (99,000 worldwide)**
Rating: **TRYING**

Written policy prohibits discrimination: **Yes, since 1990**
Includes awareness of gay and lesbian issues in training: **Starting to**
Lesbian and gay employee group: **GALAXe (Gays and Lesbians at Xerox)**
Domestic-partner benefits: **None**

The company may have (reluctantly) given its name to the language and may make a lot of other lists as a model corporate citizen, but one hears more gripes than praise from gay and lesbian employees. Seems that policy takes a long time to filter down. Suspicion is that there's resistance from some high places. Still, the employee group is vital, vocal, and making progress. Now unmarried employees can bring a guest to company events, just like spouses. Doesn't sound like an invitation to dance, though.

YWCA of Greater Milwaukee ▽▽▽

Headquartered: **Milwaukee, WI**
Approximate Number of Employees: **60**
Rating: **GOOD**

Written policy prohibits discrimination: **Yes**
Includes awareness of gay and lesbian issues in training: **Yes**
Lesbian and gay employee group: **None**
Domestic-partner benefits:

Bereavement/sickness leave

Each YWCA chapter is its own autonomous corporation, so policies vary widely nationwide—and in no way resemble the attitudes of the YMCA (not good, for all that the Village People did for them). In the Milwaukee chapter, which does extensive work in race relations, openly gay employees speak glowingly of the support they get from management. An attempt to obtain health benefits was rejected by its insurance carrier. (Is that story getting too familiar?)

Ziff-Davis Publishing Co.   ∇∇∇∇∇

Headquartered: **New York, NY**
Other Major Locations: **California, Massachusetts, and worldwide**
Approximate Number of Employees: **3,700**
Rating: **EXCELLENT**

Written policy prohibits discrimination: **Yes, since the 1980s**
Includes awareness of gay and lesbian issues in training: **No**
Lesbian and gay employee group: **None**
Domestic-partner benefits:

> **Access to company events and facilities**
> **Bereavement/sickness leave**
> **Relocation assistance**
> **Health coverage (includes partner's children)**
> **Dental plan**

The computer magazine publisher (with related publication, trade show, and consumer activities) is said to have been imbued with gay-friendliness from the beginning by its founder-owner, who only recently retired. The company had an early reputation for diversity: it hired Jews at a time when other magazines wouldn't. Women, however, have had to struggle for promotions, but that's improved. To its credit, Ziff was outspoken against Colorado's Amendment Two at a time when the company was planning to move its headquarters to the Rocky Mountain State. It didn't move.

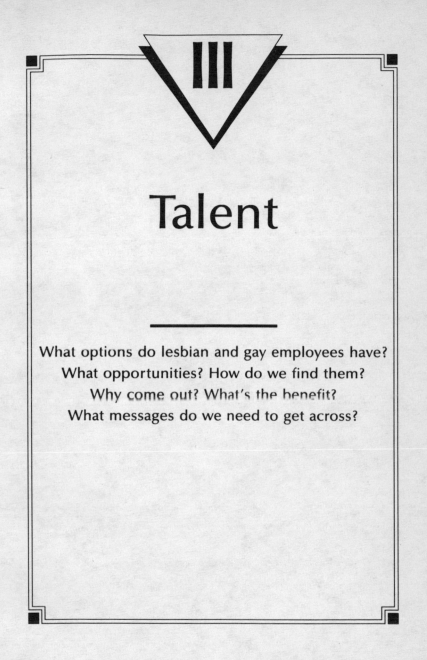

III

Talent

What options do lesbian and gay employees have?
What opportunities? How do we find them?
Why come out? What's the benefit?
What messages do we need to get across?

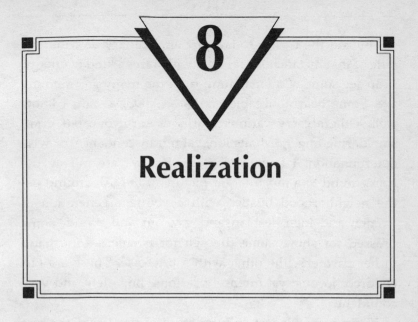

Realization

In this legendary gay mecca, there is a vague sense of change in the cool summer air. Not downtown around my hotel, where the small pink triangle on my suit lapel draws strange, sometimes hostile looks from tourists and staff alike. But ride the Muni up to Castro Street, that gay-mecca-within-the-gay mecca, and notice something different. It still looks the same. Here, over the past decade, it was difficult to walk without the eerie sensation that the place was thick with ghosts. That feeling was found nowhere else, not even amid the more personally painful blocks of New York's Christopher Street, a spot equally devastated by holocaust.

But on the Castro today, just an ordinary day, there is little of that melancholy. It hums with a fresh kind of energy. I can see some of it emanating from the many gay men my age. Some bear noticeable marks of AIDS, a sight I know well. Others carry various marks of survivors: old grief, smoldering anger, exhaustion, calm transcendence, or wise determination. I know these too. But we are mostly the background to a much larger picture of life. All around us, the neighborhood bustles with a younger generation of women and men, lesbian and gay, out and proud, some dressed for show, some dressed for business—one hand in her partner's, the other with a briefcase. These are our children. Joyous, yet intensely serious. Impatient and very confident.

This is the biggest cultural story of the 1990s, the one bursting through in theater, literature, the visual arts, even chewing its way through the censored boundaries of television and film. It's also one of the biggest business stories of the 1990s, one of changing expectations. But that hasn't begun to sink in yet.

I'm in San Francisco to make a half-day presentation on lesbian and gay employment issues to the national diversity council of one of AT&T's many divisions. This is part of an ongoing program to educate members about the many aspects diversity can have in the workplace. It's more than the standard "Gay 101" I usually have to deliver—answering misconceptions, breaking down stereotypes, offering facts to counter long-held prejudices, cajoling an audience to look at new possibilities. This time it's a savvy group. They want me to go "in depth," and I'm prepared with facts and figures and documents and exercises. I had submitted a proposal. They had liked it.

The tradition of this group is to do something "extra" after a presentation. The morning half of the day I speak will be devoted to Asian issues; for lunch, they'll all go to Chinatown. After my presentation, it's been arranged to go to the Castro and do something "theatrical." I ask about dinner. I'm told that no one could really think of anything in terms of "gay cuisine." I concede. (I avoid mentioning the politically correct alternative of something macrobiotic; I'm no great fan myself.) The word "quiche" is mentioned, bravely. I hesitate, then agree to laugh. These folks are okay.

At a reception the night before I'm set to speak, I meet the woman who will give the Asian presentation. She's prepared the way I am, but has an extra dimension about Asian culture: she has tapes of Asian music. One of her exercises will be tai chi. She tells me this is what they asked for.

I'm caught off guard. I find the group's organizer to ask if I've misunderstood. "Oh, no," he reassures me. "We didn't ask that from you. We figured there really wasn't anything equivalent, like *gay culture*."

Uh-oh, I mutter to myself. You've missed this boat entirely. They think being gay is all about sex. And apologizing for it. That's how we get sidetracked in workplace discussions. The workplace isn't about sex. But it is about *who we are*. About the experiences we have that shape us, that are different from what non-gay people know. The language that we share among ourselves to describe those experiences, good and bad. The world we have that is so tightly interwoven into the mainstream, yet so subtly distinct.

There may be nothing so monolithic as a gay culture or

a lesbian culture, but there has to be a way I can describe what I have seen on Castro Street. It's just as legitimate as any other culture. And it certainly has an effect on business and how we behave in the workplace.

I realize I'll be up half the night revamping my presentation. I'll need props. There's little time or technical equipment. But there is a tape deck. I'll use music. Except all my own tapes are back home. I zip over to the big music store up the street. Ah, there she is: my beloved k.d. lang. She'll make the point about what it means not to change the names or the pronouns. But what else? Too confusing to have to tell the stories of Tchaikovsky, Bessie Smith, or Cole Porter. We've been writing and performing music for everyone for a long time and getting no credit. Music stores don't exactly have gay/lesbian sections, not even in San Francisco.

Back up to the Castro. There's that little store that sells all kinds of items by and for local lesbian and gay organizations. They have a music shelf. I grab a concert recording of Michael Callen's Flirtations. What those guys manage to cover in an hour—issues of HIV, gender, race, all tied through good music and great gay wit—is the equivalent of a course in Gay 101. But what else?

I explain my situation to the man behind the counter. I'm sure he thinks I'm deranged. We look at various recordings of the San Francisco Gay Men's Chorus. I'm not familiar with them. Knowing (and enjoying) several other of the many choruses around the country, I'm concerned about being just a little too campy or sappily sentimental. Oh, what the hell. The salesman picks one out. The contents on the label show a mishmash of classical songs, show tunes, pop favorites, Latin (Latin?), and old chestnuts. "This," he says. "Definitely this."

I take his advice and head back to the hotel with my treasures. On the borrowed tape deck, I pop in SFGMC's *How Fair This Place* and discover something extraordinary. They have captured everything I have churning through me and much, much more.

I don't know exactly what it was: the elegant, opening oboe solo; the fact that the first sung word is "Alleluia"; the lingering over words like "still" (as in, from *Miss Saigon*, "I still believe."); the Rachmaninoff; the religious texts; the love medley (no pronouns changed) and its sudden conclusion with the multiassociational "Unchained Melody." (I am reminded of the famous publicity shot of this chorus, in which members turn away from the camera to commemorate another member lost to AIDS. Of 120, only six face forward.) Maybe it's the rousing rendition of "This Is the Moment," a great coming-out song.

More than just the individual numbers, the message is in the collection. There is no familiar self-deprecation here, nor self-pity. They have taken over powerful associations— love, loss, spirituality, tradition, hope, continuity, all aspects of our lives that are often denigrated or denied. They do it in a way that is powerful, self-assured, calm, deliberate, refined, and competent—no, flawlessly expert. Their message is "We have a right to this. So we're just taking it."

And I realize that is the real message of lesbian and gay workplace issues. We have full and complete rights to safety, acceptance, and equality. So, one way or another, we're just going to take them. If business can get past the old nonsense, there's going to be plenty of benefit to go around.

Next day, I'm primed. I start my presentation with fun music and some diversity exercises, ready to build my case. Not too far into the program, a man stops me with a question. "Don't you think," he poses quite seriously, "that homosexuality could be like smoking? If you just stopped, you'd get over it?"

There are audible gasps from some other members of the group. I stop, take a deep breath, and begin, once again, the process of Gay 101. There can be no assumptions anywhere. We have so much basic teaching to do, all of us. And I'm reminded that the script I've dreamed up has a long way to go before we can realize it.

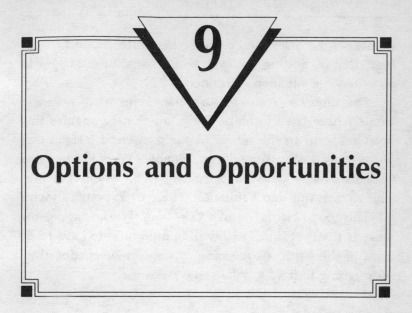

Options and Opportunities

What is so appealing about the three types of behavior— "counterfeiting," "avoiding," and "integrating"—illustrated in Woods and Lucas's *The Corporate Closet* is that they ring so absolutely true. Lesbians, as well as gay men, and anyone else familiar with us, have witnessed all three types of behavior in the workplace. Some of us have played all three parts ourselves—as a continuum that moves in only one direction. (It's difficult, practically and psychologically, to move backward.)

It's important to understand these three modes, because that's where we've been for a while. But that's not where we're going. All three are purely reactive. They may be three different choices, but they are all passive acceptance of old and unproductive "business as usual." Even "integrating" in most of the cases cited could be better described as "coping," that is, putting up (even while not shutting up) with an untenable situation. Who needs it?

The time has come to turn the tables in this no-win game. I have tried to make the point that companies that don't respond to the needs of their gay and lesbian employees are losing something valuable. We gay men and lesbians already know the price we pay. So would it be possible to turn this into a situation where everybody can win?

The good news is the answer's "yes." The less appealing news is that lesbians and gay men are going to have to do most of the work. We're going to have to keep educating. We're going to have to take some risks.

Don't Ask, Don't Get

Not one of the gay-friendly companies listed in this book got that way without somebody asking for change. Sure, some may have been predisposed with enlightened management. Some may have been gradually prepared by a growing number of lesbian and gay employees who began to stick together and stick up for one another. Or maybe by courageous non-gay allies. But no company gets changed for the better by people who lie about themselves. Or by people who avoid truth. Even those who just cope don't necessarily make change. If one is truly "integrating" one's behavior into an existing environment, one should expect certain concessions. Such as safety, acceptance, and equality.

Every gay-friendly company starts with (at least) one person who stands up and says, "I need to see a clear statement of policy." Or "I need support to deal with fear, ignorance, and prejudice." Or "I want the same access to benefits as everyone else." It's not enough just to come out. You've got to start a dialogue. You've got to be clear about what you want. And expect to get it.

This takes courage. I know, I did my time in corporate America too. We are still at a point in history where there are few role models to show us how. We may have to *be* those role models for others.

We already know how to make excuses. We've heard so many. If you're gay and a woman or a person of color, you can hide behind your fears of a double (or triple) whammy. If you're a white man higher up the corporate ladder, you may feel you have a greater responsibility to the sensitivities of the company, the clients, or your own bank account than to your own well-being or that of other gay men and lesbians. (There's an irony in the term "position of responsibility.")

Now, it's not my intention to criticize the choices people make in their personal or professional lives. If you are content in your current situation, personally and professionally, then you should let it work for you. However, if you're not content—and from what I've seen and heard around the country, more and more lesbians and gay men are not—then you need to make change. There are more options for you than ever before. That is, if you'll start with the first choice: coming out at work.

Power

Before all the binding fears kick in, I'd like to point

out that, in years of talking to lesbians and gay men in the workplace, I have never found one who regretted coming out on the job. I have checked with other researchers, trainers, career counselors, and journalists, and they have corroborated what I found. Sure, there are those who are angry at their employers or others, but they aren't angry at themselves. They know they did the right thing for themselves.

Why is that? Everyone is different, of course, and in different circumstances. There are a lot of psychological factors that get involved. But I think the two most important, in how they affect the workplace, are power and value.

Coming out in the workplace isn't much different from coming out in any other aspect of your life. It is its own reward: you feel great for being honest with yourself and with others, especially those you like. There are various ways of doing it: Dramatically, with a big splash on national television or by bringing a same-sex date to a company event (not recommended for the faint of heart). Subtly, by wearing a discreet emblem such as a lambda. (It's tough to be subtle with a pink triangle—clashes with everything.) Or you can move forward gradually, by telling one close associate, then maybe another, then your boss, then a wider circle. (Of course, the grapevine will often move faster than you.)

But whatever steps you take, you gain power. Actually, you're taking back the power you had given to others through fear. When you're being honest, no one can hold anything over you, real or imagined. (This is the root of the old "security risk" myth that even the military doesn't buy anymore.) You feel the results immediately. Less stress. More comfort (no matter what the reaction). More sense of control.

After all, what can happen? What most lesbians and gay men find (and this is somewhat anticlimactic) is indifference. Most reasonable adults in the workplace are getting used to working with people who are different from themselves. Of course, this can mask a variety of other problems, which we'll deal with later, but what matters is that these aren't *your* problems anymore. They belong to somebody else.

Often—and I do hear this a lot—you'll find more support than you would have imagined. Once you've broken the silence, you may be answering many questions that people have had about you, such as why you seemed so standoffish. They might even admire you. Of course, you'll suddenly hear from all sorts of gay and lesbian colleagues (closeted and not), who will be looking for some sort of reassurance for themselves (and hopefully not looking for a date). From non-gay colleagues, you'll suddenly hear stories about their own gay friends and family. This is intended to make you more comfortable, although it can become quite tedious.

The worst-case scenario—the one we always fear the most, the one that keeps us locked up—is one of being rejected, reviled, made fun of, and ultimately demoted or fired. This happens. But it's time to look at it in a different perspective. If that's the kind of reception coming out would get in a company, there has to be something pathological about the place to start with. If they can't deal with your difference, how are they dealing with

differences such as gender and race or religion or ethnicity or disability? How are they dealing with differences
among their *customers*? If they are so rigid or so insecure
that they can't value you for the job you do and have to
retreat to their old baggage of fear and ignorance, how
are they dealing with changes in the marketplace, in the
economy, in the world? Smug and rigid corporations are
crashing all around us. Those that can't cope, can't
change, are goners.

Why would you want to be there?

If your answer is, "It's good for my career," I suggest
you rethink that conclusion. If your answer is, "I need
the job," well, that may be the case for the short term.
But for how much longer? How much are you short-
changing yourself?

Value

Once you gain the power of coming out, questions
about your own value inevitably follow. Whenever you
put up with a homophobic comment, even one where
insult is unintended, you devalue yourself. How you react is, of course, a matter of circumstances. If you're facing ten skinheads with chains and knives, discretion may
be the better part of valor. But if it's a blowhard colleague,
or even a boss, you have every right to object. I'm not
saying you should attack. Sometimes a pained look will
do it or a simple, "Please don't use that word." (This is
precisely the kind of behavior we'd appreciate from non-
gay allies, but so rarely get. If more people did this, the

insults would drop from common usage. It's happened before.)

If a problem is persistent, you have every right to go to the next level up or even to corporate human resources. Try to explain the problem in understandable language. Sputtering "that homophobic pig!" is not always useful. You may have to explain that "faggot" is an insult whether applied directly or not, but the point is to demonstrate that an abusive manager is a bad manager, that this kind of behavior is damaging your productivity.

If the company has any sense of decency or if it values your work, management will recognize they have a problem on their hands, and it's not you. Corrective measures should be taken. If they are not, you just got a very clear message.

A homophobic comment may seem like a petty example, but just how much are you willing to put up with? Nasty messages addressed to you? Physical harassment? What? If you can't stick up for yourself in the small things, how else are you devaluing yourself? In your performance? Your potential? In your salary negotiations? And does it overlap into your personal life? Are you devaluing your relationship? Your partner?

Perhaps you're already wrestling with these questions. That's a good sign. Power brings value. If you like playing victim, you can put up with all the nonsense, convince yourself you're powerless, insult your own value, and moan about it. Or you can try another option: take a good look at what you have to offer.

Each of us have different talents. There are dozens of

self-help books and tests and programs that can help you identify yours, feel more secure in them, or find work or a career that best suits them. If you need these, you should make use of them. I bring this up only because I come across so many gay men and lesbians who look at their talent as something they have *in spite of being gay.* What's disturbing about this mind-set is that it feeds the notion that being gay has nothing to do with your work, that it is something to keep separate, to hide. That being gay is bad.

Let me propose an alternative perspective: that some of the best talents you have are yours *because* you're gay.

Difference

Lesbians and gay men are not the same as non-gay people "except for whom we sleep with." That was just an old political strategy that is no longer productive. It was never true. Men are different from women, one race is different from another, the young are different from the old, and so on. The circumstances of our lives *shape* us to be different. It's not a matter of being better or worse, just different. But nobody likes to talk about that. The forces of conformity are that strong.

It means that mistakes get made and opportunities get wasted. My friend Per Larson, the career and financial planner with a sizable gay and lesbian clientele, observes that the standard models for both careers and finances are designed to fit only one mold: that of the heterosexual married couple with children. If you differ from that description in any way, you should be looking for different guidelines.

For example, in terms of career, he points out that gay men and lesbians develop an ease of mobility from an early age—some are actually propelled from the nest or hometown because of difference. In our twenties, we have a greater opportunity to take risks, to travel, explore, continue in school, try out different jobs, socialize, spend money—in short, experiment and get experience—because we don't have to worry about feeding the baby. Career advancement need not be a priority.

The result, Larson says, is that by the time we are in our thirties, we've gained not only a high degree of education (formal and informal) but also a mastery of some highly prized business skills: mobility, risk-taking, and experience with different types of people. (He recommends this age for investing in a corporate job or jobs, for the credentials, training, discipline, networking, salary, and benefits such employment can offer.) Later, while our non-gay peers are struggling to get the kids through college, we're better equipped to switch jobs or careers, start our own businesses, or even retire early (if we've been careful financially).

Of course, this isn't the profile for every lesbian or gay man. Some of us do have children or other responsibilities, such as taking care of parents. But, I think, for most of us, there is something in the nature of gay life that does make us more open to taking risks, being prepared to move and change, being more attuned to issues of diversity. We need to recognize the value of these enhanced skills. So do our employers.

In terms of talent and skills, I'd go even further. I think we have the toughness of survivors, which is why we didn't commit suicide the way too many gay and lesbian youth do. I think we have a remarkable ability to handle stress (which the military found out in its own research—to its chagrin) simply because we're more used to hostility and uncertainty. And I think we look through a different lens at the world, as other minorities also do, but ours is enriched by the unique situation of growing up isolated from our own kind.

We may not have specific role models in the business world, but we do have role models. (Although more than a few prominent businesspeople have come out, been outed, or are "sort of known" around the community.) We find them as we uncover our long-neglected history. Gertrude Stein and Sappho, Michelangelo and James Baldwin, Tom Dooley and Franz Schubert, the Indian berdache, shaman, and medicine woman. Artists and teachers, healers and spiritual leaders. I don't mention the famous ones who are currently alive, only because I can hear the ready reaction: "Well, in their fields it's okay to come out." Not necessarily true, but this isn't about playing to stereotype, either.

Don't we have use—no, a crying need—for these skills in business of any kind? Translate "artists, teachers, healers, and spiritual leaders" into "innovators, mentors, communicators, and visionary managers." Problem-solvers. We're born to that role. From the earliest days when our difference begins to dawn on us, we set out to bridge the gap between what we know and what we're told. We explore in order to find new possibilities. We have to work every day to find creative solutions to living life with integrity.

I'll dare to suggest, at the risk of putting all lesbians and gay men on the spot, that our talents are special and much needed in the world today. I'm not claiming superiority for us. It's just that our talent and skills have been degraded and submerged for so long, it's time to champion them. Most of us already use these skills every day to our employers' benefit. If their source could be acknowledged, we might do even better. Everybody could win.

Mommy Track

Unfortunately, even among many of the gay-friendly employers listed in this book, that message has not yet sunk in. Most companies are likely to view lesbian and gay employees as a "problem" to be "dealt with" (alas for the poor human resources manager suffering from "issue fatigue") rather than assets to be cultivated. It falls to us to join with other "issues" and teach the companies what they need to know to survive and thrive. In the process, we will discover—and create—what it really means to be "out at work."

Corporations are changing, at least in part, because the workforce is changing. Over the past decade or more, there has been a growing focus on "quality of life." While some companies reduce this concept to just nicer working environments, or benefits and perks, or flextime and child care, in its entirety what it's all about is the intersection of the personal and the professional. Working women must balance career with child rearing (since we still haven't lost the sexist assumption that it's their responsibility). But increasing numbers of dads, remembering a whole generation of absentee, work-obsessed fathers, want more freedom to be an integral part of their children's lives. All kinds of people want more time to give to community work or charity or even hobbies that give them great satisfaction. Workers are willing to compromise even on money to achieve these goals. The enlightened companies that are flexible enough to strike this deal (many of whom are listed in this book) find they get considerable payback in terms of productivity and loyalty.

Although we rarely look at it this way, gay and lesbian workplace issues fit squarely into this phenomenon. (Does "intersection of the personal and the professional" ring a bell?) In our case, however, the compromise isn't always about activity, but about classification and the perceptions that go along with it.

Even in companies where the battle for safety, acceptance, and equality has been won, there is a subtle discrimination that is slightly different from the glass ceiling or "lavender ceiling." It may be based in dogged prejudice about who we are, but more likely it's rooted in concern about *what we might do.* I think the closest parallel is the "mommy track" that women have discovered. Women who choose to take time (even a short time) to have children during their careers are often stigmatized, viewed as somehow "disloyal" for not having put their jobs first, always. That assumption extends to the priorities they have to set regarding child care—school, illness, and other demands children might make. As a result, they are put (without their knowledge) on a career track that limits their advancement. Working fathers who have chosen to put boundaries on their professional lives for the sake of their children also report this kind of trade-off. But in the case of working women, being put on the "mommy track" can happen just because they are of childbearing age.

In the case of lesbians and gay men who are out at work, the issue isn't children but a fear of "activism." (Or as one human resources executive said to me, in a related context, "working to better their own kind." She quickly caught herself, apologizing, "I didn't mean that to sound condescending.") There's an assumption that you'll not only "make waves" but put a greater priority on organizing and educating than on your actual job. This couldn't be further from the truth. (Some of us *wish* that more— even just a few more—lesbians and gay men would take on that kind of work.) But I do suspect that this is why at least some openly gay men and lesbians, at companies as friendly as Levi Strauss and Digital, distance themselves from their identities out of concern for "compromising their effectiveness." I don't criticize their decisions, especially because many of these good people have been brave and admirable agents of change. But it does suggest that there are issues ahead on the frontier.

Most gay men and lesbians in the workplace are still a long way from dealing with that level of subtlety or sophistication. Most still fear for their jobs if their identity becomes known or are struggling with harassment or are shut out of the advantages their non-gay coworkers enjoy.

Many are in the process of achieving enough of a sense of self-respect and dignity, enough courage to face up to problems that have long been denied and dismissed, by both themselves and their employers. With their growing sense of courage and confidence, those dissatisfied with their situations are beginning to recognize three options: They can continue to do nothing, a tried-and-true option that seems less and less attractive. They can leave for a more welcoming and productive environment. Or they can roll up their sleeves and help their companies to change.

Voting with Your Feet

While discussing this book with a non-gay friend who has thirty years of experience in corporate human resources and in career counseling (with a special emphasis these days on "out placement"), I asked her what she thought of my belief that the best choice lesbians and gay men could make for themselves was to come out at work.

She was horrified.

I explained to her the price we pay in that fearful juggling game of keeping our identities secret—and what the company loses too. I pointed out how non-gay people use sharing bits of their personal life as a way of building better working relationships—something we lose out on when there is secrecy. I suggested that the compensation package was stacked against us and our own family responsibilities.

She reconsidered. "Actually," she said, "my first reaction was a memory of what I saw twenty years ago when I was at General Electric. I saw horrible things done to gay men. But now I'm thinking about what I always tell job hunters: a good career situation results only when there's a successful match between the company and the individual of skills and values. And this is certainly about values on both sides. Putting a gay person, out or not, in a homophobic company could be a big mistake. Especially for the individual."

In the current atmosphere of restructurings, layoffs, and a sluggish economy, every working person gets paranoid about his or her job. Business gets the advantage of keeping us paralyzed by our own fears. But how long can you live in suspended animation? If you are abused, fearful, or ignored, you need to get out of that situation before you shrivel up completely. Of course, each of us has to weigh all the factors that contribute to job satisfaction. Gay and lesbian issues are only one factor—although an important one—in a mix that includes overall quality of life, salary and benefits, opportunities to do what you do well, and other considerations. If a situation is unacceptable, with little hope for change, it's time to reach for your walking boots.

I'm not suggesting an instant mass exodus of lesbians and gay men from companies that aren't fair to us. (But that would be splendid, wouldn't it?) Nor am I suggesting that all of us should get on line at employment centers for the companies listed in this book. (They couldn't handle all of us, anyway.) But I am suggesting that each of us begin to think strategically about our own futures and look at the alternatives we have to our current way of life.

Should you choose to leave your current employer, you actually have two further choices (assuming you have to work): you can either get a new job in better circumstances or set up shop on your own. Both of these are in the finest tradition of what is often referred to as "free-market capitalism."

Entrepreneurial Flight

Lesbian and gay entrepreneurship is such a familiar and time-honored fixture in our community that it's amazing no one has yet done a thorough study of the phenomenon. Nearly every major city has a gay and lesbian business association. (The oldest, New York's now-defunct Greater Gotham Business Council, was founded in 1975. It has been succeeded by the Stonewall Business Association.) A sizable proportion, if not the majority, of their members are independent business owners. Thousands and thousands of them: bright, ambitious, imaginative. They all worked for somebody else's company at one time. Most have stories of feeling extremely uncomfortable—if not experiencing outright discrimination—from an employer. It's clearly a motivator. You have to wonder if the "somebody elses" noticed what's been lost to them.

I'm not talking just about people in stereotypical "gay professions," such as florists or decorators or hairdressers. They are there, of course. But there are also the management consultants, the public relations experts, the independent producers, the mechanics, the computer systems specialists, the restaurateurs, and the retailers. They serve an overwhelmingly non-gay clientele, which makes some of them, especially older ones, sensitive to "client perceptions." They can still control their own destinies, without the constant poison of prejudice. If a client can't tolerate you, you don't have to tolerate the client.

Not all of these businesses are small. We shouldn't forget that one of the world's most successful recording and entertainment companies and one of the most prominent business publications were built by gay men. But it is time to find a replacement for the term "mom and pop": a new breed of lesbian and gay business has been flourishing, one that provides services to the increasingly visible (and loyal) gay and lesbian community. Insurance brokers, financial advisers, opticians, chiropractors, accountants, realtors, personal trainers, publishers, hotels and resorts, cleaners. There's even an emerging field of consultants who help non-gay businesses, which have begun to notice the market, to sell to gay men and lesbians. There are plenty of opportunities. As *The Wall Street Journal* reported in July 1992 ("More Openly Gay Women Are Starting Own Businesses"), in Chicago alone, the number of lesbian-owned businesses had quintupled to more than five hundred in the preceding five years.

But how many of us really achieve that Great American Dream of being our own boss? Nobody has an answer to that yet. Well, why do we pursue the dream?

The most obvious answer is that, until only very recently, it was the most reliable path to job security for a gay person in business—even considering how risky starting one's own business really is. It still has been the best chance to have an integrated, working life of honesty and integrity. Issues of safety, acceptance, and equality are best dealt with when you yourself are in complete control of them. But there may be more to it than that: those life skills that lesbians and gay men must cultivate to survive—risk-taking, mobility, and an ability to work with different kinds of people—might adapt us particularly well to independence. For good measure, throw in a different financial responsibility pattern, stress management skills, the will to survive, and the energizing relief of freedom. These aren't everything that a start-up business needs, but they provide a pretty handy psychological foundation.

If you're a gay or lesbian employee ready to start your own business, there's plenty of technical help and general support available to you within the community and outside of it. Use it. If you have a skill or a better idea, and you're not feeling appreciated by your employer, go for it if you can. If security concerns you, you might consider negotiating a part-time job (with a current employer or a new one) until you're flying. Think creatively. Considering the trend toward downsizing, hundreds of thousands of Americans are being faced with a choice between self-employment and unemployment. But you don't have to wait for that. And it just may be possible that, in terms of self-employment, we have a head start.

If you are an employer, it's time to think seriously about the potential drain of talent out of your organization. American business doesn't have a great record for tracking the quality of the workforce; instead there's been an assumption that, like most other resources, talent will just keep coming. That's a mistake. Talent, especially the best and the brightest, needs to be cultivated. Gay men and lesbians have a lot to offer. Through prejudice, or just plain lack of attention, are you letting talent slip away? If so, you may not feel the results immediately. But you will eventually.

Finding a Gay-Friendly Company

Okay, so you're not ready, willing, able, or otherwise inclined to take the entrepreneurial route. Maybe it seems a bit extreme as a means to gaining some integrity in your work life. Whatever. If your employer or your situation has become more than you're willing to handle, you can still vote with your feet by finding a new job. The list of employers in this book is only the beginning of the possibilities.

In that 1990 article on being out in the workplace I wrote for *Business Ethics*, I quoted a lesbian executive who said, "Nobody walks into a job interview and says, 'I'm gay.' Just as nobody says, 'I've been divorced three times.'" But today I'm not so sure that is the right equation. You can have three failed marriages—or long-term relationships—whether you're heterosexual or not. While some people may view this as a character flaw, I'm not so sure that most will. But I am sure that it is no indicator of whether you can successfully perform a job.

Nor is being gay. But being gay is an entirely different matter. Nobody harasses the multiply married—except a few pinheads, who might direct such behavior at women only, and that has a different meaning altogether. How many times you've been married *is* a matter of privacy, pursued only by the prurient. It's one of those leftover Victorian judgments about "moral character," like how an unmarried man isn't likely to make it to the executive suite. (The standard often changes for women. The unmarried, sexless "career woman" is an old business cliché.) Sure, these prejudices persist. But now that we've even elected a multiply married president (in 1980), there's good reason to doubt how seriously the idea is taken anymore.

What's really different about being gay is that most lesbians and gay men *want* to say "I'm gay" in a job interview. It's a critical way of finding out what kind of working conditions or career opportunities they'll have. But, of course, few do. They're afraid.

So how do you find out?

For help with this question, I consulted several career consultants, recruiters, and job-placement specialists around the country. Most were lesbian or gay themselves, some with a heavily gay clientele because of their own prominence in their local communities. I figured they would have a handle on the issue.

To my disappointment, they did not. In fact, most advised their gay and lesbian clients to *avoid* the issue. On a purely pragmatic, immediate level, they were right, I suppose. But this is exactly how we perpetuate our own closet. This is how we ensure that fear and prejudice will persist.

The brightest light I found in this picture came from

Joe McCormack. Capping a distinguished career as an executive recruiter for America's top corporations, in 1992 Joe founded McCormack & Associates in Los Angeles, the first executive-recruiting firm to specialize in recruiting top-notch *openly gay* management talent. Granted, the level he deals in is pretty rarefied, and his clientele is corporate and organizational, but I knew we were on the right track when he told me he asks potential candidates, "What is it worth to you to live a life of integrity? To be the same person to all people?"

Joe frankly admits that being openly gay or lesbian can limit career opportunities, especially in certain industries such as mining or oil and gas. But he balances that with the observation that changes in attitudes toward diversity, recognition of markets, and better understanding of gay and lesbian issues are opening up new opportunities all the time. While he advises corporate clients not to make the mistake of tokenism and to hire only the best candidate, he reminds candidates to look at the whole complex picture of a job offering. The goal is to make a suitable match. (I'm reminded of "skills and values" here.) But he often suggests that candidates do a thoughtful career inventory: looking at how being out—or being closeted—has limited or enhanced career goals.

As for finding gay-friendly companies, we both agree that the state of research has changed dramatically since the old days of just five years ago. Traditionally, word of mouth was the only source of information. (It certainly raised the status of companies such as Levi Strauss and AT&T.) Today more companies are willing to open up their own closets (for a variety of reasons) and be known as gay-friendly employers. Books (such as this one), newsletters, electronic bulletin boards, all types of media coverage, and ongoing research (such as that being conducted by the Workplace Project of the National Gay and Lesbian Task Force) are just beginning to compile this information. But it's only a start. And the situation keeps changing rapidly.

There are many thousands of employers in this country alone, and on most of them lesbian and gay job candidates are going to have to do a lot of their own research. The information may be gathered during interviews or by snooping around the organization, but it doesn't have to involve a great deal of risk.

The most important area to explore is simply that of attitudes. The prevailing corporate culture will give away much about its stance toward gay and lesbian issues, even if they're not talked about. (This can be a pretty subjective topic, so get more than one opinion. There are optimists and pessimists in all companies.) If there are the heavy handprints of some conservative, old, white, male dinosaurs, you may have to wait for them to die out. (Unless they're just going to be replaced by younger versions of themselves.) This can reveal itself in a rigid or smug attitude toward marketing, technology, or employee relations—look for the insistence on the explanation "This is how it's done." If there are signed pictures of Pat Buchanan or Jesse Helms on the wall, take the hint. If the company is family owned and operated, it can go either way. If it's gay-friendly, that often means someone highly placed has done the groundwork for you. If there's a lot of emphasis on "we're just like family here," you might be cautious about just how much con-formity that demands. If you hear "family values," just run.

If you're a woman or a person of color or disabled, it will be expected that you'll ask questions in these areas. If you're a fully able white man, you should ask about these issues anyway, since they might provide a clue about whether people are valued for what they do, rather than any other criteria. (If there's surprise that you asked, take note.)

Ask about employee groups, what kinds there are, if the company welcomes them, what such groups do. This might connect well into talk about policies (such as non-discrimination) and what gets covered in training pro-grams (if there are any). If there are domestic-partner benefits, you'll certainly hear about them when benefits are discussed.

A slightly tougher challenge will be looking for role models. If there are no openly gay or lesbian employees, you may have to rely on gay radar. If all you can pick up is closeted nervousness, this may reflect more on the individuals than the company. The ideal situation is to find a lesbian or gay employee who you can talk with. You should note whether that person is in a "stereo-typed" job—especially if you're not. And, of course, if you sense anything predatory, you should look into how sexual harassment issues are dealt with.

Once you've explored this kind of background and you've weighed just how good a deal you might get there, you can always choose to be direct, although it's recom-mended that you wait until the end of the interview. "By the way, I'm gay. Is there any problem with that?" is one way to put it. If there isn't, you'll know immediately. If they've already made you an offer and there is a problem, you should talk it through with them and others. If they withdraw an offer, depending on where you're located, you could consult an attorney.

Does coming out in a job interview sound too far gone to you? Then you're probably not ready to do it. But consider, if we don't start asking the question, employers aren't going to get used to hearing it.

Besides, only a direct statement provides any degree of certainty. No organization is perfect or consistent. Should you have any problems later, at least you'll know if you have written policy to back you up, or whether you can rely on support from someone in a position of authority. If you wait to come out later, after you've started on the job, you're still running a risk of business as usual or of starting the hunting process all over again. Or making change in the company.

Making More Gay-Friendly Companies

Ultimately, the only goal we can have as gay men and lesbians is to make every company gay-friendly. While this is an agenda that is sure to put opponents of change into a tizzy, it's a goal we owe to ourselves and the generations to come. Maybe someday business will even realize its value.

Changing the law and the opinions of the electorate isn't enough, as women, African-Americans, and others can attest. The task is larger than that. We're going to have to teach industry by industry, company by company, individual by individual.

Happily, the process is well under way, and it's not as mysterious or foreboding as some might fear. All the employers listed in this book have been through it or something similar to it or are undergoing the process now. You can initiate it where you are now or select a new employer where circumstances better suit you.

I've already outlined the basic issues companies need to be aware of—safety, acceptance, and equality—and how to address them: in policy, education, and benefits. Now I'd like to set out an action plan for lesbian and gay employees and our allies.

The preliminary step is that you recognize the value of your own talent. If you can't appreciate it, few others will. And talent is the single most important negotiating tool we have.

COME OUT

Obviously, nothing can be expected to change unless the problem becomes tangible. Anti-gay initiatives succeed best when we are an abstraction. That's why they need us to remain silent. Don't collaborate. Make it personal. Tell your own stories and experiences. These are the most powerful educational tools we have.

There's risk here, since it's impossible to anticipate how people will react. What matters most is that you come out in a way that's natural for you, that's consistent with your own standards. Don't let anyone tell you there's only one way. Just be honest, and follow your own comfort level. If you're harassed, keep notes. Document everything. Then bring it to your boss, your boss's boss, or to the human resources manager. To your union, if you're a member. Or call corporate headquarters. If it doesn't take you seriously, you may have other options. If you're in a protected jurisdiction, you might consult your state or city human-rights commission. If you're not, you might consider going public. Get help.

Please note: If you work or live in a place where coming out may be physically dangerous, be realistic. Be careful. We need you alive. Give those of us in safer environments a little more time to make progress. (Please note, those of us in safer environments!)

BAND TOGETHER

Once you've started the coming-out process, you're likely to find out you're not alone. Reach out. Create a network; if possible, form a group. If it has a friendly social atmosphere, it's more likely to develop a healthy dynamic of its own. But don't overlook the importance of support. People should feel comfortable talking about their concerns and problems. It's crucial that you respect one another's choices, especially about coming out. Be sensitive, too, to our own differences, such as gender, race, religion, lifestyle, and perhaps most important in this situation, position in the organization. You don't need a clique. You need a united front.

GET STRATEGIC

As individuals and as a group, begin to identify problems. Look for patterns. Then think creatively: develop specific goals or solutions to the problems. It's more fun (and productive) than whining. Each workplace is different, but hopefully this book has provided some ideas to start with. Depending on where the employer is on a gay-friendly scale, you may need a non-discrimination policy, or enforcement of one, to deal with harassment. Also desirable is inclusion in training programs that deal with other forms of discrimination. Maybe it's time for a reexamination of benefits policy.

This is also an ideal time to start doing your homework—it'll come in handy later. Teamwork helps a lot here. Get the latest versions of company policy. Take part in training programs. Ask questions. If your need is for equal benefits, learn the details of the existing benefits policy. Find friends in the human resources, benefits, and legal departments—if you don't already have members there—so they can help you understand the intricacies. Also, find out what other companies are doing, especially other companies in your industry or profession. Get copies of their policies. They are exhibits-in-waiting.

COMMUNICATE

Get out and around the company and start making allies. They don't have to be gay, just supportive or at least helpful. This isn't so much about numbers as about cultivating assistance in valuable places. You can keep it informal at this point, since you're still learning. Make the group's case to the diversity manager, if there is one—that person should be familiar with some concepts from literature in the field. Ditto human resources and benefits, if they are separate functions. Definitely talk to union representatives, if any unions are involved (and if this won't completely freak out management). If you're really thinking ahead, you might start talking with folks from communications and marketing; they will be essential for getting your message out to the rest of the company. And later, when fears start surfacing about an organized backlash. If you're really lucky, you might find a senior executive somewhere (gay or not) who's willing to act as a mentor.

If other employee groups already exist (such as for women or racial groups), I can't emphasize enough the value of building bridges to them. In all likelihood, you'll have members in common (though they may not come forward). Most important, other groups have already been through much of the process you're about to go through, such as getting acknowledged by the company, opening dialogue, influencing training policy, and so on. You don't have to reinvent the wheel. They'll probably gladly share their own experiences and methods. And you'll probably be able to return favors later.

PRESENT A PLAN

Since the whole organization is probably buzzing by now, it's time to go official. First, have the group do itself a favor by choosing one or two articulate members to serve as spokespersons. The chief point here is that too many voices can blur the impact of the message. Also, given the hierarchical nature of most companies, having only one or two contacts will simplify communication—it will probably make the powers-that-be more comfortable. They may even take you more seriously.

Then sit down together and make a plan of action: What do you expect the company to do? What are the most pressing problems? What steps should come first? What later? You might ask for a non-discrimination policy first, then recognition of your group. Group participation in training is a logical next step. Approach benefits gradually, starting first with no-cost or low-cost items such as partner access to company events or facilities. Then work your way up.

The most successful action plans that I've seen (such as at Apple) are those that take a gradual steps approach. Don't lay all your expectations on the table at once. That's a good way to alienate important potential allies. Remember, you're educating. Start simple, gain trust, and open up a continuing dialogue. It works.

When you're ready, set up an appointment with the highest-ranking official you can, preferably the CEO. If the company is really huge, the director of human resources will do. Your highest-ranking allies will probably be the most help here, both in selecting whom to talk to and getting the appointment. Send only your designated spokespersons. They should keep the presentation short and to the point. State the problems. Suggest the solutions. Show the documentation and exhibits you've been collecting. Don't talk about human rights, no matter how passionately you feel. Keep strictly to business issues: productivity, morale, loyalty, the law. For the first meeting, present only what you think is essential. Then listen. Somebody else may be appointed as a liaison to your group. Don't worry, it probably means you have your collective foot in the door.

EXPECT RESISTANCE

You're not going to get an immediate response to any-thing. Sometimes we forget, because we live with them all the time, how new lesbian and gay issues are to most other people. Their first reaction may be to resist some-thing they don't understand. Be prepared. Have answers. You may have to give everything time to sink in.

That's internal resistance. Expect external too. Militant heterosexuals within the company probably won't put up a direct objection to your requests. Most will be too ashamed or afraid of being perceived as bigots, especially in contrast to your courage. Their approach is usually to alert an outside fundamentalist group, which can then start cranking out the letters and activating the phone trees.

Even if this doesn't happen, management may fear it will. Here's where allies in communications and market-ing will prove invaluable to allay that paranoia. They will know how to present change both within the company and outside to the media. They will know the company's markets and be able to tell whether an attack will have any real effect or if it's just a lot of noise.

BE PATIENT

Depending on the size and complexity of the organi-zation, change can take time. Remember, this is a long-term process. Be open to negotiating, if that's what it takes. But obviously there are some areas that don't have room for compromise. Either a company permits dis-crimination or it doesn't. Either it advocates tolerance and acceptance or it doesn't. In terms of equality—well, that's where it can get complex, because money is involved. You can still stand on principle. You're the petitioner, but you're also the talent. Do they know what you're worth? If you've come this far in the process, they probably do. And if they don't, it's time for you to show them that *you* do.

Looking Beyond

When I think it through, I have no trouble believing that the lesbian and gay goal of achieving safety, acceptance, and equality in the workplace will be achieved, and quickly. Unlike so many other arenas of life, where the numbers are against us, the workplace gives us a chance for a clear-cut bargain: our talents in exchange for respect. And we indisputably have so much to offer.

But sometimes I try to figure out where the workplace issue fits into a larger scheme. (Friends like to make fun of me as a "big picture" kind of guy.) I can see it as one of the great—and maybe one of the last—frontiers of the gay and lesbian rights movement. Because it's one we've been so afraid of for so long. Because it's such an important aspect of life. Because it brings with it almost unimagined opportunities for us to correct prejudice and to show our real worth.

Sometimes I see it as an arena in which, for once, we *all* see a tangible, immediate value. It's something we can each work for in our diverse, creative styles, and see the benefit accrue to all of us and each of us. As we make progress, each of us changes for the better. I see so much energy and optimism released by this workplace stuff, I almost believe we, such valuable agents of change, could accomplish anything.

Could we change business? Capitalism? Society? Humanity? Maybe. I find myself going back more and more to the still-unanswered questions posed more than forty years ago by Harry Hay and the philosophers of the early Mattachine Society: "Who are we? Where have we come from? What are we here for?"

We—gay men and lesbians, and the society that produces us, for whatever reasons—must begin to work together to remove the barriers that disable our enormous potential. The challenges we all face, on a global scale, are formidable. But the problems can be solved. And our special skills, experiences, and outlook—our talents—will hold the key to many of them.

It's time to get down to business.